THE BATTLE OF WISCONSIN HEIGHTS 1832

THE BATTLE OF
WISCONSIN
HEIGHTS
1832

THUNDER ON
THE WISCONSIN

PATRICK J. JUNG

THE
History
PRESS

Published by The History Press
Charleston, SC 29403
www.historypress.net

Cover image: Portrait of Black Hawk by Charles Bird King (from Thomas L. McKenney and James Hall, *The History of the Indian Tribes of North America*, 1836–1844).

First published 2011

ISBN 978-1-5402-2961-8

Library of Congress Cataloging-in-Publication Data

Jung, Patrick J., 1963-
The Battle of Wisconsin Heights, 1832 : thunder on the Wisconsin / Patrick J. Jung.
p. cm.
Includes bibliographical references.
ISBN 978-1-5402-2961-8
1. Wisconsin Heights, Battle of, Wis., 1832. 2. Black Hawk, Sauk chief, 1767-1838. I.
Title.
E83.83.J85 2011
977.5'03--dc22

2010053830

To Katherine, Aloysius and Francis

Contents

Acknowledgements

I first learned about the Black Hawk War as a young boy, and ever since I have sought to learn as much as possible about this fascinating conflict. That interest prompted me to write a doctoral thesis, an earlier book and several articles on the Black Hawk War. I have also delivered public lectures and paper presentations on this topic at scholarly conferences.

Several persons and institutions deserve thanks for assisting me in this endeavor. First, I want to thank Father Francis Paul Prucha, SJ, and Dr. Alice Kehoe for kindling my scholarly interest in American Indian history and culture during graduate school and encouraging me to research this subject. My alma mater, Marquette University, provided generous grants and fellowships during my years of graduate study; much of the research that I did during that time went into this book. That research would not have been possible without the assistance of the staffs of various libraries and research institutions, particularly the United States National Archives, the Marquette University Library System, the Wisconsin Historical Society, the Milwaukee Public Library and the University of Wisconsin–Milwaukee Golda Meir Library. Most of all, I want to thank my parents, Robert and Georgia, for their constant encouragement and support, and my wife, Rochelle, for her many years of unconditional love. Finally, I want to thank my children, Katherine, Aloysius and Francis; this book is dedicated to them.

Introduction

The story of the Black Hawk War of 1832 is an oft-told saga in northern Illinois and southern Wisconsin, where it was fought. It is a story of chicanery, duplicity, savagery, heroism and even redemption. It was the last Indian war fought in this region, and when it was over, the United States took the land from the Indians (under the guise of legitimate purchase) and then sold it to white settlers who came to live on soil that once belonged to the Sauks and their confederates, the Foxes. The leader of this war, the great Sauk warrior Black Hawk, ended his days not on the lands he fought in vain to preserve for his people but in a new country farther west in present-day Iowa, where the federal government forced his tribe to move. During the brief war he led against the United States, he saw half of the people under his leadership killed in the savage massacres that characterized many of the war's battles. Indeed, for Black Hawk and his surviving followers, the war cast a black shroud over their collective memories of that time.

Yet this dismal outcome cannot obscure the superb military leadership that Black Hawk demonstrated during many phases of the war. His crowning glory occurred at a place called Wisconsin Heights, a precipice along the Wisconsin River with two distinct hilltops, one to the north and one to the south. Black Hawk chose the southern of the two prominences to make a stand along with a mere 120 warriors against an estimated 700 American militia volunteers. Given these numbers, Black Hawk knew he could not win; that was never his goal. His objective was to hold off the American forces long enough so that the remainder of his followers—women, children and the elderly—had enough time to cross the Wisconsin River and put this wide obstacle between them and the white volunteers. While greatly outnumbered and taking horrific casualties, Black Hawk achieved this difficult end. It was, without a doubt, the high point of his career as an Indian war leader.

It is this battle, the Battle of Wisconsin Heights, that is the focus of this book. Located near the cities of Sauk City and Prairie du Sac in south-central Wisconsin, the site of the battle is today preserved as a state park and historical site. One can still walk the ground that Black Hawk's warriors and the volunteers trod as they engaged in combat on that fateful day of July 21, 1832. The hilltop where Black Hawk commanded his forces is a high, rocky prominence studded with gnarled pines. Standing atop this high point, it is easy to see why Black Hawk made his stand here. It affords an excellent view of the northern hilltop where the volunteers took their positions, as well as the Wisconsin River, below which Black Hawk's people made a desperate retreat across the waters. Anyone walking on these hills today can almost hear the thunder of the muskets, the cries of the wounded and the soft whispers of the dead.

This book presents an accurate and detailed account of this tremendous battle. For residents of south-central Wisconsin, this volume has a special significance because the Battle of Wisconsin Heights is woven into the fabric of the region's history. Indeed, Sauk City and Prairie du Sac take their names from the Indian people known as the Sauks who lived in the immediate region about one hundred years before the battle and who, under Black Hawk, fought, bled and died at the Battle of Wisconsin Heights. For readers interested in the military history of the Black Hawk War, this book provides a narrative of the one true, large-scale battle of the conflict. The others—Stillman's Run, the Battle of Pecatonica, the Battle of Bad Axe, etc.—were small raids and skirmishes, unorganized retreats or outright massacres. Only at the Battle of Wisconsin Heights did both sides employ the classic stratagems of fire and maneuver using relatively large bodies of men.

Before the story of this battle can be told, it is necessary to look at the early history of the Sauks, their confederates the Foxes and other tribes such as the Kickapoos, Potawatomis, Winnebagos (also known as the Ho-Chunks) and Menominees who found themselves, often unwillingly, tangled in the web of events that led to the Black Hawk War. It is also critical to examine the events that transpired in the wake of the Battle of Wisconsin Heights, particularly the sad and disturbing story of Black Hawk's people, who, in the weeks afterward, suffered starvation and bloody massacres at the hands of the United States military forces. Still, the Battle of Wisconsin Heights stands as the focal point of this narrative, for despite all of its bloodiness, tragedy and horror, the battle provides a story that also includes heroism, drama and courage.

The Midwest and the Great Lakes

Lake Superior

CANADA

Drummond Is
Mackinac Is

Lake Huron

MICHIGAN TERRITORY

Ft. Snelling

Green Bay
Ft. Howard

Mississippi Rv

Prairie du Chien
Ft. Crawford

Ft. Winnebago

Lake Michigan

MICHIGAN TERRITORY

Ft. Gratiot

Saginaw Bay

Cedar Rv

Ft. Armstrong

LEAD MINING REGION

Detroit

Malden

Lake Erie

IOWA

Galena

Chicago
Fort Dearborn

Saukenuk

Fort Meigs
Fort Stephenson

Ft. Madison

Prophetstown

OHIO

Missouri Rv

Cuivre Rv

Springfield

INDIANA

St. Louis
Jefferson Barracks

Ohio Rv

MISSOURI

N

The Midwest and the Great Lakes. *Map produced by the author.*

1

Origins of the Black Hawk War

The Black Hawk War, in a sense, started when Europeans settled the North American continent. In the early 1600s, the Sauk tribe lived in the Saginaw River Valley in the lower peninsula of Michigan, while the Foxes (who called themselves the Mesquakies) lived nearby in southern Michigan and northeastern Ohio. It was at this time that the French established settlements in eastern Canada. Both the Sauks and Foxes spoke the same language within the Algonquian language family and once had been a common people (along with the Kickapoos) several centuries earlier. The Five Nations League, composed of Iroquoian-speaking tribes in New York, attempted to dominate the Great Lakes fur trade with the Europeans in the 1640s and 1650s by annihilating other Indian communities in the region and in the process pushed these tribes and others westward. By the end of the 1600s, the Sauks and Foxes lived in northeastern Wisconsin.[1]

Later, some Foxes returned to their original homeland in southern Michigan and became embroiled in hostilities with tribes allied to the French. About one thousand Foxes died in an armed clash with these tribes near the French outpost of Detroit in 1712, thus precipitating a twenty-year series of conflicts with the French known as the Fox Wars. By 1732, the French had reduced the tribe to a mere two hundred souls, all of whom sought refuge the next year with the more populous Sauks at Green Bay. This began what would be a long period of political confederation between the two tribes. While they retained separate political structures, the Sauks and Foxes coordinated their external relations with European powers and other Indian

Sketch of Pontiac, Ottawa chief and leader of Pontiac's Rebellion. *From* History of Jo Daviess County, Illinois, *1878.*

communities. Indeed, the appellation "Sauk and Fox" became the term by which others referred to these two distinct yet allied tribes. The French launched a final genocidal war against the Foxes and their Sauk allies in 1733, but both tribes managed to escape farther west toward the Mississippi River. After a final, failed campaign in the winter of 1734–35, the French, unable to achieve their military goals, made peace. The two tribes remained in the Mississippi River Valley for the next century and had village sites that stretched from the Des Moines River in the south to the Wisconsin River in the north. The Sauk village of Saukenuk, one of the largest, stood at the confluence of the Rock and Mississippi Rivers. It was here that Black Hawk was born in 1767. By the early 1800s, the Sauks had a population of about fifty-three hundred, while the Foxes, who slowly recovered from the Fox Wars, had a population of about sixteen hundred.[2]

The French lost control of North America after the French and Indian War from 1754 to 1763. Like many tribes in the Midwest, the Sauks were initially leery of the British. Some of them, along with Ojibwa allies, participated in the massacre of the British army's garrison at the Straits of Mackinac in 1763. This was part of a larger, loosely coordinated set of uprisings known as Pontiac's Rebellion led by an Ottawa chief from Detroit by the same name. The British soothed the hard feelings the war caused by reestablishing the system of trade that the French had developed. This system allowed the Indians to have political and cultural autonomy within the lands over which the French and later the British claimed suzerainty in exchange for allegiance and peaceful trade. In the period after Pontiac's Rebellion, the British established control over Canada and the American Midwest; France gave its vast colony west of the Mississippi, known as Louisiana, to Spain as a reward for its support during the French and Indian

War. Almost immediately after this conflict ended, the American Revolution began. When the war was over, the new United States assumed control of the former British lands that stretched from the Great Lakes in the north to the Florida panhandle in the south and the Mississippi River in the west. The British retained control of Canada, and Spain continued to exercise dominion over Louisiana. During these decades, the Sauks and Foxes found themselves in the very uncomfortable position of having to carefully balance their external relations with these three competing powers. For example, in 1780, during the American Revolution, the British forced the Sauks to attack St. Louis (then in Spanish Louisiana) because Spain had allied with the United States. The Sauks mounted only a halfhearted, unsuccessful attack. Their poor performance displeased the British, but it nevertheless angered the Spanish and the Americans, and a month later a combined Spanish-American force attacked Saukenuk.[3]

In the end, however, the United States would be the source of the greatest number of problems for the Sauks and Foxes. This was because the United States, unlike France, Britain or Spain, did not seek to establish a loose empire in the vast expanses of North America in which the Indians could continue to live as they always had as long as they traded their valuable furs for goods of European manufacture. The United States was willing to administer its new western territories in this manner for a short period, but this was seen merely as a transitional phase. Ultimately, the United States wanted to purchase the Indians' land by what were known as land cession treaties. Often, the Indians negotiated these treaties in a position of weakness vis-à-vis the United States. Thus, they were often coerced into "voluntarily" selling their land. The federal government then forced the Indians to leave in order to make room for white settlers. This was the case with the Indians of the Ohio country. These tribes fought against the United States in the Northwest Indian War from 1785 and 1795. The Indians lost and were forced to cede the Ohio country to the United States by the 1795 Treaty of Greenville. Indians farther to the west, such as the Sauks and Foxes, watched these events with concern, for they rightly feared that the United States might make them the next victims of this insidious policy. Black Hawk was a young man at the time, and he expressed the sentiments of his people when he stated that "we had always heard bad accounts of the Americans from Indians who had lived near them!"[4]

The Sauks and Foxes became targets of this policy much sooner than they expected. The leader of France, the imperious Napoleon Bonaparte, decided to establish a new French empire in North America. In 1802, he secretly purchased Louisiana from Spain. This sent shivers down the spine of President Thomas Jefferson, who feared having an aggressive European power directly across the Mississippi River from the relatively weaker United States. Jefferson decided that the United States needed to purchase Indian lands on the east bank of the Mississippi in order to counter possible French aggression. Thus, in 1802 he instructed the War Department (which had responsibility for Indian affairs) to purchase southwestern Illinois from the Kaskaskia Indians; the land cession treaty effecting this transaction was signed in 1803. That same year, Jefferson concluded the purchase of Louisiana (better known as the Louisiana Purchase) from Napoleon, thus precluding the need to buy additional Indian lands. However, he wanted to ensure that no other tribes had claims to the lands ceded by the Kaskaskias. Thus, in June 1804, his secretary of war instructed William Henry Harrison, the governor of Indiana Territory (and later the president of the United States for a month), that "it may not be improper to procure from the Sacs [*sic*], such cessions on…the southern side of the Illinois [River], and a considerable tract on the other side."[5]

Portrait of Indiana territorial governor William Henry Harrison. *From Frank E. Stevens,* The Black Hawk War, *1903.*

Origins of the Black Hawk War

It was with this broad mandate that Harrison set the events of the Black Hawk War in motion. Harrison arrived at St. Louis in October 1804 to govern the upper districts of the Louisiana Purchase. United States soldiers had taken possession of St. Louis, and the Sauks and Foxes were disturbed by this change of governance. Even worse, Americans began to establish settlements on what the Sauks insisted were their hunting grounds. One such settlement popped up about thirty miles northwest of St. Louis on the Cuivre River. In September 1804, a party of four Sauk warriors killed three white settlers there. This attack did not have the sanction of the tribal leadership, and to prevent retaliation by American soldiers, a delegation of four Sauks and one Fox went to St. Louis in October with one of the perpetrators to meet with Harrison, whom they hoped might extend clemency to the young warriors. In a way he did, but it was not what the delegates had in mind. Jefferson wanted to obtain Indian land for the growing United States, but he wanted purchases to be conducted in a just and humane manner. Harrison had no such scruples and aggressively sought to swindle the Indians out of their territory by any means. What happened during the course of Harrison's meeting with the delegates is sketchy because no journal of the proceedings remains. The Sauk civil chiefs Pashipaho (The Stabbing Chief) and Quashquame (Jumping Fish) had been given the authority by the Sauk tribal council (and probably by the Fox council) to gain pardons for the perpetrators; they were not authorized to sell land. Also, the negotiation of land sales normally involved the entire leadership of a tribe, not a small, five-man delegation. Harrison agreed to pardon the perpetrator, who accompanied the delegates (and who now languished in prison), as well as his accomplices, in exchange for a land cession from the Sauks and Foxes. Harrison also dispensed whiskey and kept the delegation drunk during the deliberations. On November 3, 1804, the delegates signed the treaty, which ceded most of western Illinois, southwestern Wisconsin and a strip of eastern Missouri to the United States. For these fifteen million acres of land, the Sauks and Foxes received $2,234.50 worth of goods immediately and a perpetual annuity (or annual payment) of $1,000 in trade goods.[6]

It's tempting to say that Harrison completely hoodwinked the delegates and that they had no idea the treaty sold their tribes' land to the United States. However, the Sauk and Fox delegates probably were told during the negotiations that they were selling some land in exchange for freeing the young Sauk who accompanied them, as well as gaining pardons for the others involved in the Cuivre River killings. The question remains about how much and what land they thought they were selling. Quashquame asserted that the delegation had only sold a small bit of land north of St. Louis; this was an area used as hunting grounds where the two tribes had no permanent villages. This almost certainly would have met with the approval of both tribal councils since it would have ended the controversy over the Cuivre River affair. In later years, Sauk and Fox tribal members acknowledged that the delegates had sold land to the United States. However, it is clear in the

Sauk and Fox Land Cessions and Tribal Locations

Sauk and Fox land cessions and tribal locations. *Map produced by the author.*

Origins of the Black Hawk War

Portrait of the Shawnee Prophet.
*From Thomas L. McKenney and
James Hall,* The History of the
Indian Tribes of North America,
1836–1844.

historical records that they did not know how much of their country had
been sold, and over time, as they gradually came to understand that virtually
all of the two tribes' domain had passed into the hands of the United States,
the Sauks and Foxes expressed shock and outrage. Quashquame asserted for
the rest of his life that he had never knowingly sold any land north of the
Rock River—these were the most valuable and populated of the Sauks' and
Foxes' country. To make matters worse, the young warrior held as a prisoner
did not even live to see his freedom. He was shot dead while reportedly
attempting to escape his captors. The entire sordid episode did much to
increase the mistrust that the Sauks and Foxes already harbored against the
United States. Later in his life, Black Hawk complained that the 1804 treaty
"has been the origin of all our difficulties."[7]

The Sauks and Foxes did not have to leave immediately. The federal
government first had to survey the land and open it for settlement, and that
did not begin until the late 1820s. However, a series of tumultuous events
occurred between the 1804 treaty and the 1832 Black Hawk War that

exacerbated an already tense situation. The first began in the Shawnee lands to the east in present-day Indiana. There, in 1805, an Indian prophet arose by the name of Tenskwatawa, or "The Open Door." He is better known as the Shawnee Prophet. After receiving a vision from a supreme deity he called the "Master of Life," Tenskwatawa preached that Indians must lead virtuous lives and eschew the evil cultural trappings of white men. Except for firearms, a strict prohibition of the white man's wares, particularly alcohol, was to be observed. He was not the first such Indian prophet, for Neolin (better known as the Delaware Prophet) had preached a similar message in the 1760s that sought to give Indians a sense of racial solidarity in their ongoing conflicts with whites. The Shawnee Prophet's message, however, was not aimed at whites in general; it was aimed at Americans in particular. Moreover, it spread like wildfire among the Indians of the trans-Appalachian West, including the Sauks and Foxes. After 1808, the Shawnee Prophet resided at a village called Prophetstown at the confluence of the Tippecanoe and Wabash Rivers in Indiana, and Indians from as far away as Lake Superior came to hear his teachings. A significant number of Sauks and Foxes made the pilgrimage to Prophetstown. A party of 240 Sauks passed through his village in May 1810, and 1,100 Sauks, Foxes and Winnebagos arrived in June 1810. Many of them spread his message to other tribes. Whereas the Shawnee Prophet promulgated a religious message, it was his brother, Tecumseh, who used it to forge a political alliance among the

Sketch of the Shawnee Indian leader Tecumseh. *From* History of Jo Daviess County, Illinois, *1878.*

Indians west of the Appalachians. Tecumseh had fought in the Northwest Indian War and was later determined to stop the sale of all Indian lands to the United States government.[8]

The efficacy of the Shawnee Prophet and Tecumseh became evident in many tribes as strong anti-American factions arose that sought to translate the Shawnee brothers' message into tangible action. This was particularly true of young warriors, for among the Indian tribes of the trans-Appalachian West, men gained social esteem primarily through great feats of bravery in battle. In the autumn of 1805, young Sauk and Fox warriors killed two white settlers in Missouri and another in present-day Iowa and later threatened to attack an American military detachment sent to arrest the perpetrators. In 1807, a Sauk warrior killed a white trader at Portage des Sioux in Illinois. The Sauks and Foxes were not alone, for young warriors from other tribes, particularly the Winnebagos, were also zealous adherents of the Shawnee Prophet and Tecumseh, and along with their confederates among the Kickapoos, Iowas and Potawatomis, they stole horses, killed livestock and attacked white settlers in Illinois and Missouri.[9]

American officials blamed the British in Canada for inciting the Indians against the United States, but the reality was far different. The United States and Britain had a tense relationship after the American Revolution. The British in Canada feared that the Americans might try to conquer their colonies in Canada. This was hardly a product of paranoia since the new United States had attempted, during the War of Independence, to seize the province of Quebec. While this attempt failed, the British nevertheless continued to cast a suspicious eye on their former colonial charges. Indeed, the Indians were not puppets of the British during the early 1800s; they were allies who had many of the same goals. Both the British in Canada and the Indian tribes of the trans-Appalachian West had a vested interest in preventing American expansion into their territories. Moreover, from 1807 onward, the British and the Americans began to drift toward war. The British in Canada sought allies for this coming conflict. Thus, the British maintained strong political relations with the tribes, particularly those in the United States. British agents invited Indians from lands under American sovereignty to Canada, where they lavished them with presents such as cloth and firearms. Malden, the British post across the St. Clair River from Detroit, was one of the principal meeting sites. Sauk parties regularly visited Malden.[10]

Both the British in Canada and their Indian allies went to war against the United States, and it was the Indians who delivered the first blow. In the autumn of 1811, William Henry Harrison, in his capacity as the governor of Indiana Territory, moved an American military force within a few miles of Prophetstown. Indian warriors present in the village (many of whom were Wisconsin Winnebagos) attacked on the morning of November 7, 1811. In what is known as the Battle of Tippecanoe, Harrison earned lifelong fame (and the nickname "Tippecanoe") when he routed the Indian force. The battle was not decisive, however, and the Indian warriors at Prophetstown, inflamed by the martial spirit this first battle provided, dispersed throughout the Midwest with an even more intense hatred toward the United States and began to commit small-scale attacks against American frontier settlements. Congress declared war against Great Britain seven months later on June 18, 1812, yet during this period the United States was forced to fight an undeclared war against the Indians. William Clark, who became famous for the journey of discovery he undertook with Meriwether Lewis several years earlier, now was the governor of Missouri Territory, and he recorded at least fifty attacks by Sauk and Fox warriors against the livestock, crops and homes

Painting of Fort Madison, produced about 1808. *From Frank E. Stevens,* The Black Hawk War, *1903.*

of American settlers in his immediate vicinity. A favorite target of the Sauks was the small American military post established in 1808 at the junction of the Des Moines and Mississippi Rivers named Fort Madison. Black Hawk and other Sauk warriors participated in a surprise attack against the fort in 1809, and with the commencement of hostilities in 1811, the Sauks and Winnebagos began to openly attack the post in the spring of 1812. The Indians killed one American soldier and destroyed several buildings outside the fort's walls. The situation for the small garrison was so precarious that the U.S. Army abandoned Fort Madison in the autumn of 1813.[11]

With the official declaration of war in June 1812, the British began to aggressively recruit Indian allies to fight alongside their redcoats. One of these was Black Hawk. In fact, virtually every Sauk warrior, along with thousands of others from tribes such as the Fox, Winnebago, Kickapoo and Potawatomi who were already inspired by the message of the Shawnee Prophet and Tecumseh, savored the chance to join their British allies in a war against the United States. Black Hawk summed up these sentiments when he noted that while the Americans made many promises they did not keep, "the *British* made but few—but we could always *rely upon their word!*"[12] In 1813, Black Hawk and other Sauk warriors traveled all the way to Michigan and joined a British-Indian force in the Battle of Frenchtown near Detroit. Black Hawk later participated in the unsuccessful sieges of Forts Meigs and Stephenson in Ohio. The total number of Sauks who accompanied him probably did not exceed three hundred. The next year, upwards of one thousand Sauks and perhaps hundreds of Foxes participated in a more significant series of battles in the Sauk and Fox homeland. In May 1814, the United States, determined to secure a military presence in the region, attempted to replace Fort Madison with a new military installation at Prairie du Chien. A combined force of over five hundred Indians and British volunteers from Mackinac Island subdued this garrison a few weeks later in July. That same month, the United States sent a relief expedition from St. Louis in another attempt to garrison its fort at Prairie du Chien, but it turned back when it was attacked by four hundred Sauks, Foxes and Kickapoos. Sauk women even participated by boarding the flatboats and attacking the American soldiers with their hoes. A month later, in August 1814, the United States sent another military force up the Mississippi under the command of Major Zachary Taylor, who, in addition to later serving as president of the United States, fought in the Black Hawk War. Taylor

Portrait of Major
Zachary Taylor. *From
Frank E. Stevens,* The
Black Hawk War,
1903.

sought to burn Saukenuk in retaliation for the attack on the earlier relief expedition. He was forced to retreat with his tiny 320-man force when 30 British volunteers from Prairie du Chien, assisted by more than 1,200 Indian warriors (most of whom were Sauks and included Black Hawk), forced him to abandon his proposed raid.[13]

Thus, long before the Black Hawk War, the Sauks and Foxes not only developed a strong hatred for the United States but also had tasted battle against their American foes. The War of 1812 ended with the Treaty of Ghent in 1814, and the actions by federal army officers and Indian agents in the succeeding years only increased the bitterness of the two tribes. The British negotiators at Ghent demanded that the United States not exact revenge on Britain's Indian allies; thus, the United States negotiated a series of peace treaties with these Indians. However, even as these treaties with the Sauks and Foxes were being discussed, warriors from both tribes continued to commit depredations against white settlements. The Foxes, who had a sizeable faction that advocated ending the hostilities, signed a treaty of peace with the United States in September 1815. The Sauks were far more obstinate and did not conclude their treaty until May 1816. Black Hawk was one of the signatories of this treaty, but little did he know that the United

States continued to practice deceit, for the first article of the 1816 treaty (as well as the fourth article of the 1815 Fox treaty) stated that the Sauks and Foxes, without reservation, accepted the provisions of the earlier 1804 treaty. This second act of deception only further increased anti-American sentiments among the Sauks and Foxes, and Black Hawk thundered that the 1816 treaty was "the first time, I touched the goose quill to the treaty—not knowing, however, that, by that act, I consented to give away my village."[14]

The die, for all practical purposes, had been cast, but sixteen years and other events were to transpire before Black Hawk took the fateful step of countering the two treaties. In the years after the War of 1812, the United States regarrisoned the upper Great Lakes and upper Mississippi River Valley. Before the war, there had been only three American forts in this vast region, with a mere 185 soldiers. After the conflict, the War Department reestablished these forts and built others. The five principal installations were Fort Howard at Green Bay, Fort Crawford at Prairie du Chien, Fort Dearborn at Chicago, Fort Snelling at present-day Minneapolis and Fort Armstrong at Rock Island (which was only a few miles from Saukenuk). Yet, these five forts had a combined strength of only 769 men by the end of 1822. Commanders, well aware of this obvious weakness, developed a strategy to deal with any potential Indian uprisings. In the event of hostilities, the small garrisons were to hold out only long enough for reinforcements to arrive from other posts. Militia volunteers from the local population could also be employed when necessary to bolster the manpower of the regular army soldiers. This strategy, while less than perfect, was used to good effect in subsequent Indian rebellions, including the Black Hawk War. Moreover, the United States had good reason to believe future rebellions were in the offing. The regional tribes, particularly the Sauks and Winnebagos, continued to harbor large anti-American factions. The British, rightly concerned that another war with the United States might occur, continued to maintain strong political and military alliances with tribes residing within the United States. The British maintained their post at Malden, and after the war they established another at Drummond Island, a mere forty-five miles from the American fort at Mackinac Island. Both sites became magnets for those Indians. In 1818 alone, almost 3,000 Indians visited Drummond Island, and a staggering 4,500 went to Malden. While some of these Indians resided in Canada, most came from lands under American sovereignty. Indeed, of the 5,906 Indians who received presents at Malden in 1827, 4,409, or about

75 percent, came from the United States. British agents had to perform a delicate balancing act; they wanted to keep the tribes in Britain's diplomatic orbit but didn't want them initiating hostilities against the United States and provoking an unnecessary war into which Britain could be drawn. This often resulted in the Indians receiving mixed messages of maintaining their belligerence against the United States but without commencing hostilities.[15]

Subsequent events illustrated this phenomenon. Whites, after 1815, began to settle on the rich mineral lands in northwestern Illinois and southwestern Wisconsin. The town of Galena, Illinois, on the Fever River (now the Galena River) became the central mining town in this booming region, which soon swarmed with small lead mining settlements. While the federal government sought to control this process with an orderly system of leasing, many whites mined lead illegally on Indian land. By 1826, there were about 1,500 white miners in the area, and this created friction with the local Sauks, Foxes and Winnebagos, all three of whom also mined lead in order to barter it for trade goods. This bred resentment, especially among the Winnebagos, two-thirds of whom were staunchly anti-American; in fact, they had been so ever since they had fallen under the spell of the Shawnee Prophet and Tecumseh. Throughout 1819, the Winnebagos sent red wampum belts to other tribes, particularly the Santee Sioux. Acceptance of such a belt signaled a willingness on the part of the accepting tribe to join the other in war. Nothing came of these initial efforts, for many tribal members (primarily the older, more conservative leaders) were reluctant to enter into another war with the United States, particularly without British support. Nevertheless, several Winnebagos from the Rock River area resorted to violence. Fort Armstrong became the locus of resistance in April 1820, when three Winnebagos, without the consent of their chiefs, killed and scalped two soldiers outside the protective walls. Winnebagos from the Wisconsin River region committed the next act of violence in 1826 when they killed a French family near Prairie du Chien. The crime was most likely motivated more by theft than anti-American sentiments, but its consequences led to the most significant Indian revolt since the War of 1812. The army housed the perpetrators at Fort Crawford. When the post closed due to flood damage, the garrison moved to Fort Snelling in October 1826 and took the two Winnebago prisoners along. In the summer of 1827, the tribe heard that the army had turned over the two men to local Ojibwas, who killed them. While this rumor was untrue, it came at a time when white miners were

Portrait of Red Bird. From *Thomas L. McKenney and James Hall,* The History of the Indian Tribes of North America, *1836–1844.*

overrunning Winnebago lands, and along with the lingering anti-American sentiments, many Winnebagos believed that the time was ripe for a war against the United States.[16]

Winnebagos of the Mississippi River and the Wisconsin River bands led the effort to create a new pan-Indian alliance and sent messages to the Sauks and Foxes, but at the time, only the Santee Sioux in present-day Minnesota expressed any interest. The leader, Red Bird, was a Winnebago from the Mississippi River bands, who, along with two accomplices, killed a fur trader and his hired man near Prairie du Chien on June 26, 1827. Four days later, Red Bird led an attack near the mouth of the Bad Axe River against two American keelboats descending the Mississippi River after delivering supplies

Portrait of Thomas
L. McKenney,
head of the Indian
Department. *From
Thomas L. McKenney,*
Memoirs Official and
Personal, *1846.*

to Fort Snelling. Two men were killed and 4 others wounded. Roughly 150 Indians participated in this attack. Most were Winnebagos from Prairie La Crosse (present-day La Crosse, Wisconsin); a few Santee Sioux participated as well. The size of the attack indicated that this was not another isolated murder but was instead part of a larger effort, much like those orchestrated by Pontiac and Tecumseh, to launch a large-scale, pan-tribal war against the United States.[17]

The manner in which the federal government put down what is now known as the 1827 Winnebago Uprising presaged the events of the Black Hawk War, and the consequences largely doomed Black Hawk to the tragic defeat he later suffered. The two federal officials who took control of the situation were Lewis Cass, governor of Michigan Territory, and Thomas L. McKenney, head of the Indian Department, both of whom were at Lake Butte des Morts in present-day Wisconsin holding a treaty council with the Menominees, the

Winnebagos of the Fox River bands and the New York tribes that had recently migrated to Green Bay. Upon hearing of the Winnebago Uprising, Cass and McKenney alerted local military commanders at Forts Howard, Snelling and Armstrong to the threat, but these three posts possessed a combined strength of only 518 men. Jefferson Barracks had been established near St. Louis in the 1820s as a larger post that was centrally located on the frontier and could thus dispatch more formidable numbers of troops to quell Indian uprisings in the North and South. Brigadier General Henry Atkinson, who later commanded the military theater during the Black Hawk War, departed Jefferson Barracks with 500 men on July 15, 1827. He arrived at Prairie du Chien, where, two days later, he met Colonel Josiah Snelling, who had arrived from Fort Snelling with an additional 200 soldiers. Cass had arrived earlier and put together a 130-man force made up of volunteers from the local lead mines. This force was commanded by Henry Dodge, another man who played a crucial role in the Black Hawk War and, more significantly, the Battle of Wisconsin Heights five years later. While Cass directed the war effort at Prairie du Chien, McKenney worked with the commander of Fort Howard, Major William Whistler, whose small force of about 100 regular army troops was reinforced by 51 civilian volunteers from Green Bay, as well as a 62-man company composed of New York Indians who were at the Butte des Morts council. A final contingent in Whistler's eclectic force was a company of 121 Menominee warriors.[18]

The climax of this military campaign, in the end, proved to be quite anticlimactic, for the uprising ended without further bloodshed. The Winnebagos concentrated their forces at the Fox-Wisconsin portage. In late August 1827, Whistler's force moved from Green Bay, while Atkinson led those forces that assembled at Prairie du Chien. The Winnebagos, outnumbered and outgunned, decided to surrender Red Bird and two of his associates on September 3, 1827. During the surrender ceremony, Red Bird maintained a stoic appearance, his face covered in red, green and white paint. He wore a collar of blue wampum decorated with panther claws. The regular army troops from Fort Howard stood on one side in a line, while the Menominees and the New York Indians formed another. A small military band played Pleyel's Hymn. With this act, the 1827 Winnebago Uprising came to a peaceful, if somewhat inglorious, end.[19]

In the wake of the rebellion, McKenney noted, triumphantly (although inaccurately), that there were no more "Pontiacs or Tecumthes [sic] to form and lead on confederated bands."[20] In fact, Red Bird was simply a latter-day Pontiac and Tecumseh, albeit a much less successful one. The notion that pan-tribal alliances were the key to preventing European and American expansion, by Red Bird's time, was already almost a century old, and it was a powerful set of ideas. Black Hawk was simply the next leader to attempt such an ambitious program. However, Black Hawk would only be marginally more successful, and his lack of success was due, in part, to the fact that the United States took several steps after the 1827 Winnebago Uprising to ensure that any future Indian revolts met a similar fate. In August 1827, the War Department ordered that Fort Crawford be regarrisoned. Most significantly, the army established a new military post at the Fox-Wisconsin portage, in the heart of the Winnebagos' country, that bore the name Fort Winnebago.[21]

The Sauks and Foxes did not participate in the 1827 Winnebago Uprising, which, upon first consideration, might seem odd given the tribes' anti-American proclivities. This was because the Sauks and Foxes were enemies of the Santee Sioux and, by extension, the Mississippi Winnebagos, with whom the Sioux were allied. The various Winnebago bands developed regional alliances with other tribes, and this often led to divided loyalties among them. The Sauks and Foxes had intermarried with the Rock River Winnebago bands, while the Mississippi Winnebago bands intermarried with the Santee Sioux. The tribal rivalries that were evident during the 1827 Winnebago Uprising became even more pronounced in the years that followed, particularly during the Black Hawk War. The Sauks and Foxes had moved westward into the hunting grounds of the Santee Sioux in the early nineteenth century; this produced enmity between them. The Ojibwas' wars against the Santee Sioux (for largely the same reasons) started in the 1730s, and this common enemy made the Ojibwas natural allies of the Sauks and Foxes. The westward expansion of the Sauks, Foxes and Ojibwas led to the formation of two alliance systems that became more entrenched in the 1820s and 1830s. The Sauks and Foxes and the Ojibwas were the core of the first alliance, which also attracted the Kickapoos, Iowas and confederated bands of the Potawatomis, Ojibwas and Ottawas of the Illinois River and the western shore of Lake Michigan. These tribes fought against the Santee Sioux, the largest member of the second alliance that also included the Menominees and the Winnebagos of the Mississippi bands.[22]

While Tecumseh and the Shawnee Prophet had preached against war between Indian communities, this aspect of their doctrine rapidly faded after the War of 1812. As the tribes came under increasing pressure from American settlers, they were pushed westward and came into competition and conflicts with other tribes, particularly over hunting territories. The Shawnee brothers' message was not dead, and the idea of putting aside such differences in order to create pan-tribal alliances to thwart American expansion still burned in the minds of many Indian leaders. Nevertheless, this dream was a shadow of what it had once been. In Red Bird and Black Hawk's time, only factions of tribes and not whole tribal communities united in such alliances, and the tribes often saw their Indian enemies as more of an immediate threat than the Americans. Intertribal warfare between the tribes of the Midwest generally was characterized by small war parties of ten to fifty warriors who sought to gain prestige through acts of martial bravado and avenge wrongs suffered at the hands of other tribes. These "private" wars, which often lacked tribal sanction, stood in marked contrast to "national" wars, which involved hundreds and even thousands of men from entire tribes and had the blessings of the tribal governing councils.

The federal government had a vested interest in preventing private wars since these often blossomed into national wars that spilled over and posed a threat to white frontier communities. Thus, in 1825, the federal government hosted a treaty conference at Prairie du Chien that sought to place the tribes within well-defined, agreed-upon boundaries that would be respected by all tribes and would put a damper on intertribal warfare. The peace generally held over the next three years, but in August 1828, a Santee Sioux war party killed six Ojibwas in the upper Mississippi Valley. The next year, the violence spiraled out of control when Sauk and Fox warriors attacked the Santee Sioux, and by the next year, 1830, the Menominees and Winnebagos were once again assisting the Santee Sioux. Attempts to stifle the fighting failed utterly when, during a hastily organized peace conference in May 1830, a war party of roughly fifty Santee Sioux and Menominee warriors killed fifteen members of a Fox delegation near the Fever River.[23]

However, the worst outrage occurred the next year, for the Foxes were keen to avenge the egregious crime that had occurred on the Fever River in 1830. On July 31, 1831, a one-hundred-man war party composed mostly of Foxes and a few Sauks killed twenty-six Menominees encamped peacefully at Prairie du Chien. News of the massacre even reached President Andrew Jackson, who was particularly aggrieved by the fact that the killings occurred within sight of the walls of Fort Crawford. Federal Indian agents went to great lengths to urge the Menominee tribal leaders to forestall any new acts of violence, and while the tribal leaders were willing to comply, they made it clear that they wanted the Foxes and their confederates, the Sauks, punished.[24]

It is ironic that, at the time this massacre took place, the first phases of the Black Hawk War had begun. Yet American officials were far more concerned with stemming the tide of intertribal warfare, which had the potential to ensnare white settlers who resided in frontier regions. Lewis Cass, the new secretary of war, expressed these exact sentiments when he stated that such intertribal rivalries might very well result in "a border warfare, from which our citizens would not be exempted."[25] Yet these intertribal rivalries played a significant part in the conduct of the Black Hawk War, for the United States exploited these tribal rivalries in its efforts to defeat Black Hawk. Indeed, while white militia volunteers shouldered the majority of the burden in defeating Black Hawk's band of followers, Indian allies participated in many of the battles, including the Battle of Wisconsin Heights.

2

The 1831 Standoff and the Early Weeks of the War

The immediate events that caused the Black Hawk War began in 1828, when Thomas Forsyth, the Sauk and Fox Indian agent, advised the Sauks and Foxes to leave the lands outlined in the 1804 treaty by the spring of 1829. As they had done in the past, the tribal chiefs asserted that they had never sold any lands north of the Rock River and refused to move across the Mississippi. Nevertheless, there was a definite split within the two tribes, particularly the Sauks, over the best policy to pursue. Many tribal members, sensing that resistance was a dangerous path to travel, were willing, albeit reluctantly, to abide by the treaty's provisions and establish new village sites in the Iowa country. A rival faction among the Sauks refused to budge.

In 1828, Black Hawk had not emerged as the leader of this faction. It was led by Red Head, Bad Thunder and Ioway. The federal government proceeded to survey the 1804 treaty cession and began to sell the land in 1829. White settlers were so eager to gain these lands that they did not wait for the government to finish this process and took illegal possession of the Sauks' lands. In the autumn of 1828, the Sauks departed on their winter hunts. While away from Saukenuk, Black Hawk heard rumors that illegal white settlers (or squatters) had moved into his lodge. He traveled ten days and returned to Saukenuk to learn that the rumors were true. When the remainder of the Sauks returned in the spring of 1829, they found that squatters had torn down their lodges and fenced off their cornfields. These acts prompted Black Hawk to join the anti-removal faction, and he soon became its most influential and prominent member. He and other Sauk

Sketch of Keokuk. *From George Catlin*, Letters and Notes on the Manners, Customs, Condition of the North American Indians, *1841.*

leaders met with Forsyth and discussed the situation. Forsyth remained unbending and reiterated that the Sauks and Foxes must leave their ceded lands. He also reminded Black Hawk that he had signed the 1816 treaty, which restated the terms of the 1804 treaty. Black Hawk told him bitterly that "the White people were in the habit of saying one thing to the Indians, and putting on paper another."[26]

After the meeting, another Sauk, Keokuk, spoke privately with Forsyth and assured him that most of the Sauks and all the Foxes had already moved across the Mississippi. Not surprisingly, Keokuk at this time became the leader of the pro-removal faction. It would be wrong to depict Keokuk as an American lackey. Like every Sauk, he disagreed vehemently with the 1804 treaty. In 1829, when the United States attempted to purchase more of his tribe's land, Keokuk flatly refused and made a stinging reference to the 1804 treaty when he noted that the United States "cheated my Grand Father…and we are not going to be taken in, in that way."[27] Nevertheless, he saw little point in resisting the United States; like all Indians in the region, he had witnessed how quickly the United States assembled the overwhelming military power needed to subdue the Winnebagos in 1827. He had also toured the eastern United States in 1824 and saw how numerous the Americans were as he visited cities such as Baltimore, New York and Philadelphia. In fact, federal officials regularly invited Indian leaders to the East for just that reason. They believed that one of the best ways to prevent Indian uprisings was to awe the Indians with the size and vast population of the United States. Significantly, Black Hawk did not accompany Keokuk on this tour, but he would make a similar journey in 1833.[28]

Neither Black Hawk nor Keokuk were civil chiefs, but the political dynamics of the Sauks and other regional tribes provided other avenues for leadership that were often more powerful than that of civil chief. Day-to-day governance among the Sauks and Foxes devolved upon civil chiefs who gained their positions through their paternally inherited clan affiliations. Among the Sauks, the Bear and Fish clans provided civil chiefs, while among the Foxes the Bear clan alone had this honor. Black Hawk, as a member of the Thunder clan, and Keokuk as a Fox clan member, could not become civil chiefs. However, another important position was that of war chief, which men of any clan could attain by great bravery in battle. A man had to first become a warrior, which status Black Hawk had attained by the age of fifteen when he wounded his first enemy. He killed and scalped an enemy Osage shortly thereafter and participated in his first scalp dance, whereby the enemy scalps taken in battle were displayed prominently upon a pole. These acts allowed him to wear eagle feathers and war paint and to organize his own war parties for private wars. The most respected warriors became war chiefs through merit rather than heredity. Keokuk gained his status by becoming an orator, yet another significant leadership position. Civil chiefs often had others speak for them in councils, particularly those who had a gift for communicating the spoken word. Keokuk was exceptional in this regard.

There also existed the position of band leader. Bands within tribes were loosely organized and generally went off together on winter hunts, although bands also served other purposes. Anyone from any clan could join a band, and usually the most charismatic male member became its leader. Bands had both civil and war chiefs, but the position of band leader required

Sketch of the Winnebago Prophet. *From George Catlin,* Letters and Notes on the Manners, Customs, Condition of the North American Indians, *1841.*

no recognized political or military rank. Among the Sauks, those who gravitated toward the pro-removal faction became members of Keokuk's band, while those who resisted removal became members of Black Hawk's band. Because of their anti-American sentiments (and their pro-British proclivities), Black Hawk's followers constituted what became known as the British Band. Black Hawk, however, only managed to attract about eight hundred Sauks to his standard. The vast majority (about forty-five hundred) became members of Keokuk's pro-removal faction.[29]

Black Hawk also collaborated with a half-Sauk, half-Winnebago mystic named Wabokieshiek, or White Cloud. He was better known as the Winnebago Prophet. While many whites saw the relationship between the two men through the same prism they viewed Tecumseh and the Shawnee Prophet, the Winnebago Prophet played a smaller role than his Shawnee counterpart. He had family ties to the Rock River Winnebago bands (which resided very close to his village site), and because his father had been a Sauk civil chief, he was regarded as a civil chief among the Sauks. Less is known about his religious teachings than about those of the Shawnee Prophet, but the Winnebago Prophet was nevertheless part of a pervasive religious phenomenon among the Indians of the trans-Appalachian West that stretched back over the course of the previous century. Like all Indian prophets, he professed to have contact with the spirit world and attracted disciples from various tribes (particularly the Winnebagos) in northern Illinois and southern Wisconsin.

Unlike the Shawnee Prophet, the Winnebago Prophet initially preached a message of healing and salvation rather than resistance to American expansion. What changed his thinking were the hordes of white miners illegally taking valuable lead ore from the land of the Rock River

Winnebago bands. By 1828, he still professed peace, but he increasingly expressed dissatisfaction over the federal government's failure to control this volatile situation. When Black Hawk first consulted with him during the winter of 1828–29, the Winnebago Prophet counseled persistence rather than resistance and told Black Hawk that if he stayed at Saukenuk, he would not be troubled by the Americans. He repeated this message to Black Hawk over the next several years. The Winnebago Prophet most likely provided this advice because he had heard (almost certainly from British Indian agents in Canada) that under the provisions of the Treaty of Ghent at the end of the War of 1812, the United States had agreed to recognize the rights of all tribes to their lands. While this was true, the Treaty of Ghent did not invalidate or in any way modify the provisions of the 1804 treaty. Nevertheless, the Winnebago Prophet continued to preach that if the British Band remained at peace in Saukenuk, it would in no way be molested by the United States.[30]

Black Hawk's other principal advisor was a young civil chief named Napope, or The Broth. During the winter of 1829–30, Black Hawk learned to his dismay that a fur trader at Rock Island, George Davenport, had purchased over twenty-four hundred acres of the Sauks' land on the east bank of the Mississippi, including those lands where Saukenuk stood. Napope advised Black Hawk to kill all the American officials in the region, as well as Davenport and Keokuk. This was indicative of Napope's impulsive nature, and he consistently provided Black Hawk with poor advice. It was about this time that Namoett, another civil chief who was a member of the anti-removal faction, died. This had the unfortunate effect of strengthening the hand of the reckless Napope. Moreover, two other leaders of the anti-removal faction, Ioway and Bad Thunder, also died. While this solidified Black Hawk's leadership over the British Band, it also deprived it of its most experienced leadership.

There were other developments that had a direct impact on the Black Hawk War, the most significant of which occurred in 1830, when about two hundred Kickapoos from southern Illinois joined the British Band. Like the Sauks of Black Hawk's band, these Kickapoos were members of the anti-removal faction of their tribe fighting to remain on the east side of the Mississippi rather than following their people westward across the great river. This significantly increased the strength of the British Band. These Kickapoos remained with Black Hawk until the bitter end in 1832 and played a significant role during the Battle of Wisconsin Heights.[31]

In the autumn of 1830, Black Hawk defiantly told Felix St. Vrain, the new Sauk and Fox Indian agent, that he would return to Saukenuk in the spring of 1831 after his tribe had finished its winter hunts. Black Hawk made good on his promise and returned with his followers, as well as his Kickapoo allies. Soon other Indians, particularly the Winnebago Prophet's followers, joined him. By midsummer 1831, between twelve hundred and sixteen hundred Indians, all of whom possessed strong anti-American sentiments,

Portrait of Illinois governor John Reynolds. *From John Reynolds,* The Pioneer History of Illinois, *1887.*

joined Black Hawk at Saukenuk. It was a volatile situation, and the governor of Illinois, the Indian-hating John Reynolds, decided to take immediate action and, in late May 1831, called up militia volunteers to forcibly expel the Indians at Saukenuk. However, state governors did not have such powers since Indian affairs were a federal responsibility; thus, Reynolds's actions were of dubious legality.

William Clark, the federal official at St. Louis who retained the ultimate responsibility for Indian affairs in the region, feared that the untrained Illinois militia volunteers could possibly make an already tense situation worse. Clark informed his military counterpart, Major General Edmund P. Gaines, of the situation so as to make the removal of Black Hawk's followers a federal operation. As the commander of the Western Department at St. Louis, Gaines mounted an expedition composed of six hundred federal soldiers from Jefferson Barracks who would proceed to Saukenuk and, hopefully, convince the Indians to remove peacefully.[32]

Black Hawk consulted with the Winnebago Prophet after hearing that Gaines was en route from St. Louis. As always, the Winnebago Prophet urged

Black Hawk to stand fast. He told Black Hawk that "the Americans were at peace with the British, and when they made peace, the British required (which the Americans agreed to) that they should never interrupt any nation of Indians that was at peace."[33] A short while later, on June 4, 1831, Black Hawk met with Gaines on Rock Island. Like other frontier military officers of his day, Gaines wanted a peaceful solution; he believed that Indian wars were expensive and violent affairs that, whenever possible, should be avoided. He also knew that frontier settlers, like those who made up the Illinois militia, hated Indians and often killed them without provocation. He wanted to end the standoff, if possible, before Reynolds's militiamen arrived.

Black Hawk made his sentiments known when he arrived at the meeting with several of his warriors singing a war song. Gaines repeated what federal Indian agents had been telling Black Hawk and his followers since 1828: they must abide by the 1804 treaty, remove from their lands and find new homes across the Mississippi. Black Hawk replied sternly that "*we* had never sold our country...*we* are determined to hold on to our village!"[34] Keokuk, on the other hand, was determined to work behind the scenes to weaken Black Hawk's position. He met with Gaines privately the next day and told him that he had convinced about two hundred of Black Hawk's followers to leave Saukenuk.[35]

While these negotiations ensued, local settlers, fearing that an Indian war was inevitable, began to build small forts for protection. It was a scene that would be repeated the next year. Gaines wanted to end the standoff without bloodshed, and Black Hawk, for his part, had no intention of starting a war. He told his followers that "not a gun should be fired, nor any resistance offered. That if he [Gaines] determined to fight, for them to remain quietly in their lodges, and let him *kill them if he chose!*"[36] The standoff continued for another three weeks, and many of Black Hawk's followers, sensing that they would not be allowed to remain and growing weary of the confrontation, left Saukenuk until only two-thirds of the original numbers were left.

About 1,450 Illinois men answered Reynolds's call and volunteered to serve in the brigade of militia volunteers under his command. The volunteers, who wore no uniforms and who carried a variety of arms, began their march on horseback to Rock Island on June 20 in order to rendezvous with Gaines's regular army soldiers. Gaines made a formal request for the Illinois volunteers' services on June 5, and thus they were in federal service and under his command. The Illinois volunteers certainly were not as well trained or equipped as the regular soldiers, but they had horses and were

Saukenuk and Vicinity, 1831

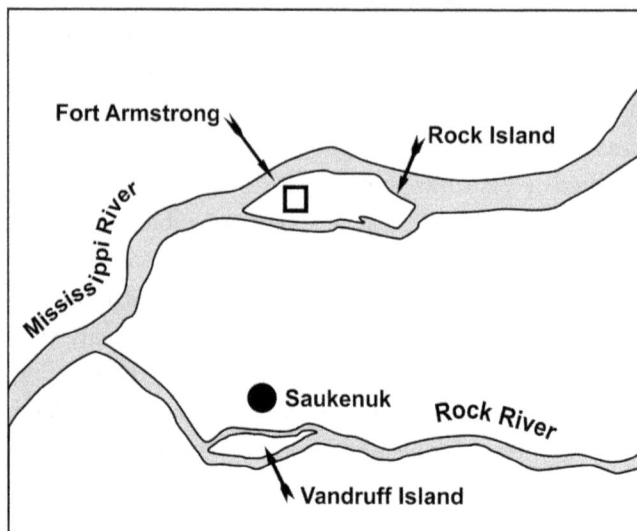

Saukenuk and vicinity, 1831. *Map produced by the author.*

mounted. Gaines had six regular infantry companies from Jefferson Barracks and another two from Fort Armstrong, but because the U.S. Army had no cavalry at this time, the Illinois volunteers provided an important element of mobility that Gaines needed in the unlikely event that Black Hawk and his followers fled and began to attack white settlements. By June 25, after a journey of 130 miles, the Illinois volunteers reached their marshalling area about twelve miles south of Rock Island and made final preparations for their assault.[37]

However, the attack never came. On the morning of June 26, Gaines was aboard a steamboat along with an infantry company and cannon, and he blasted canister shot (which made the cannon a large shotgun) into the vegetation across the Rock River from Saukenuk. He did this to cover the movement of the Illinois volunteers, who marched from the south, crossed the Rock River to Vandruff Island and then crossed a small channel onto the peninsula where Saukenuk stood. At the same time, about 270 regular army soldiers marched down the peninsula from the north after leaving Rock Island and crossing the Mississippi. When the regulars and Illinois volunteers arrived at Saukenuk, they found, much to their disappointment, that it was deserted. Black Hawk and his followers, under cover of darkness, had abandoned it the night before. Black Hawk, while confident that Gaines's regular soldiers would behave in a disciplined manner, placed little trust in the men from Illinois. He later said, "I would have remained and been taken prisoner by the *regulars*, but was afraid of the multitude of *pale faces*, who were on horseback [the Illinois volunteers], as they were under no restraint of their chiefs."[38] Black Hawk judged the situation well, for the volunteers, enraged at finding the village deserted, began to burn the Indian lodges and even desecrated the graves of deceased Sauks in a nearby cemetery.[39]

On June 30, under a white flag of truce, Black Hawk, along with Quashquame, met Gaines on Rock Island. There he signed articles of capitulation whereby he agreed to permanently remain on the west side of the Mississippi. According to an American army officer present, Black Hawk

> *arose slowly, and with great dignity, while in the expression of his fine face there was a deep-seated grief and humiliation that no one could witness unmoved...When he reached the table where I sat, I handed him a pen... He took the pen—made a large, bold cross with a force which rendered that pen forever unfit for further use.*[40]

Because his followers had been forced to leave the cornfields they had prepared at Saukenuk, Gaines agreed to provide Black Hawk and his followers with enough food to make up for this loss. When the Illinois volunteers, still camped near Rock Island, heard of this provision, they derisively labeled the articles of capitulation the "Corn Treaty." Thus ended Black Hawk's bold defiance and his futile attempt to retain his beloved homeland, at least for that year.[41]

It would have been best for Black Hawk, his followers and even the white settlers in the region if he had committed himself to abiding by the articles that he signed. His decision to withdraw from Saukenuk the night before the assault was hardly a sign of cowardice; it was, in fact, a very wise decision. There is little doubt that blood would have been spilled had he and his followers remained, and virtually all of it would have been Indian blood. Yet neither was it a sign of duplicity. Black Hawk intended, at least initially, to stay on the west side of the Mississippi; only later did he change his mind. Several events transpired over the next few months that prompted him to reassess the situation. Four weeks after he had signed the articles of capitulation, the massacre of the Menominees at the hands of the Foxes occurred at Prairie du Chien, and between fifty and sixty of the Fox perpetrators sought refuge with the British Band in order to avoid having the Fox tribal leaders hand them over to the United States for punishment. The British Band now had new members who possessed a strong desire to resist the United States.

Several months later, Black Hawk received a visit from Napope, who had visited the British post at Malden that autumn. He told Black Hawk that the British supported his decision to retain Saukenuk. Napope had also visited the Winnebago Prophet, and according to Napope, the Prophet had received from the British promises of guns, ammunition, and provisions that would be sent to the British Band via Milwaukee. Moreover, all the Indians along the western shore of Lake Michigan and the Winnebagos would join the British Band in any future attempts to resist removal by the Americans. This news almost sounded too good to be true, and, alas, it was. Indeed, Napope later admitted that the promises he had attributed to the British in Canada were nothing more than the products of his fertile imagination. Nevertheless, Black Hawk, who had suffered a tremendous humiliation during the summer of 1831, was extremely receptive to Napope's outlandish declarations; in hindsight, he simply should have been more objective in his assessment of Napope's statements. Yet as he brooded in his lodge on the west side of the Mississippi that winter, Napope's report offered him hope that he could redeem himself in the eyes of his followers. He stated, "I thought over every thing that Ne-a-pope [*sic*] had told me, and was pleased to think that, by a little exertion on my part, I could accomplish the object of all my wishes."[42]

Black Hawk used the remainder of the winter and the early spring of 1832 to recruit new members to the British Band. While he made little headway among Keokuk's followers, he had one advantage: federal Indian agents and regional military commanders remained far more concerned with preventing an explosion of intertribal warfare in the wake of the Menominee massacre in July 1831. To that end, the War Department in March 1832 ordered Brigadier General Henry Atkinson to arrest the Fox perpetrators of the massacre. On April 8, Atkinson departed St. Louis with six companies of infantry totaling 220 men. Little did he know that Black Hawk and the British Band, just three days earlier, had crossed the Mississippi in defiance of the articles of capitulation. Atkinson soon found that his mission of containing intertribal rivalries would expand dramatically throughout the spring and summer of 1832 as he chased Black Hawk through northern Illinois and southern Wisconsin. In fact, Atkinson should not even have undertaken this original mission, for his superior, Gaines, continued to command the

Western Department throughout 1832. Gaines at the time was in Memphis battling rheumatism and the flu and thus sat out the entirety of the Black Hawk War in Tennessee. Atkinson had never led troops in battle or even served in combat; his first and only time would be during the Battle of Bad Axe, the last great mêlée of the Black Hawk War. Like Gaines and other frontier commanders, Atkinson believed that preventing Indian wars was preferable to fighting them, but it would largely be because of Atkinson's actions (and incompetence) that the Black Hawk War began.[43]

On April 5, as Atkinson was finalizing his own plans and Black Hawk was leading the British Band across the Mississippi, the Winnebago Prophet met with

Portrait of Brigadier General Henry Atkinson. *From Frank E. Stevens,* The Black Hawk War, *1903.*

Felix St. Vrain and informed him that Black Hawk and his followers were headed to the Prophet's village to grow corn. The Winnebago Prophet asserted that this was not a violation of the articles of capitulation since the British Band would not reoccupy Saukenuk; because the Prophet's village was forty miles up the Rock River from Saukenuk (and on land that had not been ceded by the Indians to the United States), Black Hawk was not going back on his promise. While the available evidence is sketchy, it appears that both Black Hawk and the Winnebago Prophet hoped that such a move would be a relatively safe and calculated act of resistance (but not an act of war) that would attract the support of the regional tribes. It would also ensure the backing of the British in Canada, who, according to Napope, had already pledged their support. Black Hawk would be another Tecumseh. The Winnebago Prophet would follow in the footsteps of the Shawnee Prophet. The United States, caught off guard by this strong show of force, would have no choice but to let the British Band remain on the east side of the Mississippi.[44]

Thus, Black Hawk did not cross the Mississippi with the intent of starting a war (despite many white reports to the contrary). In fact, he sincerely sought to avoid it. The most telling evidence for this conclusion was the fact that the British Band, in addition to warriors, possessed women, children and elderly members. It was constituted as a tribal band, not a war party. It had five war chiefs and nine civil chiefs (including the Winnebago Prophet and Napope). This gave the British Band an air of political legitimacy that a mere war party would have lacked. Finally, from the time the British Band crossed the Mississippi on April 5 until it was forced to fight the first battle of the war on May 14, the actions of Black Hawk were decidedly peaceful toward the resident white settlers. Black Hawk assembled his followers at the former site of Fort Madison, crossed the Mississippi at a place called Yellow Banks (present-day New Boston, Illinois), proceeded north up the Rock River past his beloved village site of Saukenuk and traveled to the Winnebago Prophet's village. In addition to the two hundred Kickapoos who had been with the British Band for over a year, the Fox perpetrators and a small number of Illinois River Potawatomis also traveled with the British Band. All told, Black Hawk had about eleven hundred followers, five hundred of whom were warriors mounted on the band's five hundred horses. The remainder of the British Band traveled in over one hundred canoes. Ironically, as Atkinson steamed northward on his mission, he unknowingly passed by the British Band one night as it, too, was moving up the Mississippi River and thence up the Rock River to carry out its mission.[45]

When Atkinson arrived at Rock Island on April 12, he learned the full scope of the situation, but he decided to focus on his original task of arresting the Fox perpetrators. He sent a letter to Reynolds to inform him of Black Hawk's movements, and while he noted that it was not Black Hawk's intent to make war, Atkinson nevertheless believed that "the frontier is in great danger."[46] The letter did more harm than good, for Atkinson simply succeeded in fanning the flames of a fire he himself started. He consistently overstated the danger posed by the British Band and in the end did more to ensure a violent outcome than did Black Hawk's decision to cross the Mississippi. Still, Atkinson took several steps to persuade Black Hawk and his followers to return peacefully. He was only able to take three Fox perpetrators into custody; the fact that most of them were with Black Hawk put them out of his reach. Thus, persuading the British Band to return might allow him to complete two vital missions.

Keokuk and Wapello (the principal civil chief of the Foxes) also tried to persuade members of the British Band to abandon Black Hawk, but the young Fox emissary sent to deliver their message was rudely rebuffed. Atkinson instructed Henry Gratiot, the subagent to the Rock River Winnebagos, to conduct a similar diplomatic mission. He departed with a delegation of Rock River

Sketch of Indian agent Henry Gratiot. *From John Reynolds,* The Pioneer History of Illinois, *1887.*

Winnebagos, but the mission soon went awry. Upon arriving at Black Hawk's camp, the younger warriors became inflamed by Gratiot's very presence and suggested making him a prisoner and even killing him. Gratiot became so concerned for his safety that the next day he and his guides slipped into their canoes and hastened downriver to the safety of Fort Armstrong.[47]

Yet even his guides, many of whom had relations among Black Hawk's band, were engaged in a dangerous game of duplicity. Throughout the Black Hawk War, the Rock River Winnebagos, despite official pronouncements of support for the United States, aided the British Band. The same Rock River Winnebagos who accompanied Gratiot and who had professed peace, according to Black Hawk, "advised us to go on—assuring us, that the further we went up Rock river, the more friends we would meet."[48] The two most important Rock River Winnebagos to accompany Gratiot (and the two who would covertly assist the British Band during the war) were Whirling Thunder, a village chief, and the war leader and orator White Crow. The strong blood ties that existed between the Rock River Winnebagos and the Sauks and Foxes (due to their geographic proximity) meant that the Rock River Winnebagos would be some of Black Hawk's staunchest supporters. The Mississippi River Winnebago bands, on the other hand, were intermarried with the Santee Sioux, the enemies of the Sauks and Foxes, and decidedly hostile to the British Band during the summer of 1832. The Wisconsin River Bands, living in the borderland between their Rock River and Mississippi River kinsmen, were more evenly divided in their support for Black Hawk's cause.[49]

Atkinson's needless rhetoric prompted Reynolds to call for another volunteer army to remove Black Hawk's band. One of the young volunteers was a tall, twenty-three-year-old from New Salem named Abraham Lincoln, who served for a total of two months. Later in life, Lincoln boasted, with more than a touch of self-deprecation, that he was "a military hero…in the days of the Black Hawk war" who "fought, bled, and came away." Although Lincoln never saw even one hostile Indian, he noted, "I had a good many bloody struggles with the musquetoes [sic]."[50]

Reynolds also ordered the creation of two ranger battalions to perform scouting missions in northern Illinois. One of these was commanded by Major Isaiah Stillman, a militia officer. All told, Reynolds raised about 1,750 men for his main volunteer army (which assembled at Beardstown, Illinois), and the two ranger battalions brought the total number of men under arms to about 2,100. Atkinson instructed his old friend at the lead mines, Henry Dodge, to assemble another force of volunteers. Dodge was an archetype of the American frontiersman. He was born in the frontier settlement of Vincennes, Indiana, in 1792

Sketch of Colonel Henry Dodge. *From* Annals of Iowa, *1898.*

and moved as a teenager to the rough-and-tumble world of the lead mines in present-day Missouri. He attained the rank of brigadier general in the Missouri Territorial Militia during the War of 1812 and in 1827 moved to present-day Dodgeville, Wisconsin, to mine lead. By 1832, he was a colonel in the militia of Michigan Territory (to which present-day Wisconsin belonged until 1836), and his service with Atkinson in the 1827 Winnebago Uprising made him a natural choice to lead a similar volunteer force against Black Hawk. He was, in many ways, Atkinson's alter ego—decisive, aggressive and tactically competent. He also was the principal commander of the American forces at the Battle of Wisconsin Heights.[51]

While Black Hawk did not cross the Mississippi with the intent of starting a war, certain events almost ensured that violence would be the final product of his decision. Like Atkinson, Gratiot unnecessarily stoked fears when he insisted that Black Hawk "intends to go farther up Rock River—and that if you [Atkinson] send your officers to him he will fight them." Black Hawk, in his autobiography, insisted that he never said this but vowed "not to make the first attack."[52] Despite Black Hawk's declaration of peaceful intent, his warriors, it will be remembered, threatened Gratiot when he entered their camp, and herein lay the origins of the Black Hawk War. The young warriors, despite Black Hawk's insistence on peace, were eager for combat. When the Fox emissary visited the camp of the British Band, one Fox warrior who had participated in the Menominee massacre brandished a lance that he said he had used against the Menominees and now "hoped to brake [sic], or wear it out on the Americans."[53] A Sauk warrior expressed a desire to kill General Gaines, and another vowed that they would attack white settlements and then seek refuge in Canada. The white volunteers were no better. According to one of his men, Abraham Lincoln "expressed a desire to get into an engagement" so that his men could "meet Powder & Lead."[54] Later (but before the war began), Lincoln's men found an old Indian who was not a member of the British Band or even a Sauk or Fox; he was a Potawatomi. Lincoln's men accused the man of being a "damned Spy" and wanted to kill him, since "we have come out to fight the Indians and by God we intend to do so." Lincoln stepped in and prevented his men from committing what would have been coldblooded murder.[55]

Thus, it did not matter that Atkinson (despite his irresponsible statements) wanted the British Band to return to the west side of the Mississippi without having to resort to war or that Black Hawk and the Winnebago Prophet sought to make a peaceful but resolute stand to protest the provisions of the 1804 treaty. Hotheads on both sides expected and hoped for an armed conflict. Therefore, it was not surprising that the Black Hawk War started when militia volunteers came into contact with warriors of the British Band. Black Hawk continued north up the Rock River in order to gain support for his cause. The Rock River Winnebagos, initially supportive of Black Hawk, began to vacillate when they learned that a white volunteer army was now on the march. Black Hawk also met with the nearby Potawatomis. They told him that they had heard nothing about the British delivering supplies to Milwaukee. This was particularly disheartening since the British Band was running low on food.

It was at this point that Black Hawk decided that his plans lay in ruins and that he would return across the Mississippi. Ironically, it was also at this time that Major Isaiah Stillman's men had established their camp at Old Man's Creek only a few miles from the camp of the British Band. Black Hawk sent a three-man party with a white flag to let the volunteers know that he and his people would peacefully return to the west side of the Mississippi. Stillman's volunteers responded by seizing the three men. Black Hawk sent a second party of five men to cover the first party, and when Stillman's men spied them, they opened fire and killed two. They also brazenly shot one of the three Sauk prisoners in their possession. Thus, the Illinois volunteers fired the first shots of the Black Hawk War.

The surviving warriors of the second party escaped and alerted Black Hawk, who took 40 warriors and began to move toward the volunteers' camp. Soon, they encountered Stillman's full battalion of 281 men charging at a gallop. Black Hawk deployed his warriors, all of whom fired in

Photograph of Major Isaiah Stillman. *From Frank E. Stevens,* The Black Hawk War, *1903.*

disciplined volleys. Stillman's men, many of whom were drunk, began a retreat that soon became a full-fledged rout. The men of Stillman's battalion did not even stop at their camp but continued to retreat to the safety of a small settlement known as Dixon's Ferry about thirty miles to the southwest. In the end, none of Black Hawk's warriors were killed; his only battle deaths were the 3 Sauks murdered by the Illinois volunteers before the battle even began. Stillman's battalion suffered a total of 12 men dead. Humiliatingly, Stillman's rangers had been defeated by a force about one-seventh of their size.[56]

It is easy to assign blame for this fiasco, which soon came to be called, derisively, Stillman's Run. First, Atkinson, when he issued his initial orders, had the volunteers lead the movement. These orders did not include Stillman's battalion, because unlike the rest of army, it had assembled at Dixon's Ferry rather than Beardstown and had not been mustered into federal service. Nevertheless, it was an incompetent action on Atkinson's part because he was willing to let untrained, poorly led militia volunteers make the first contact with the British Band rather than his disciplined regulars. He did not even travel with the Illinois volunteers but instead marched with his regulars, who were already under the leadership of an experienced officer, Major Zachary Taylor. The Illinois volunteers who had assembled at Beardstown were commanded by Brigadier General Samuel Whiteside, and because they had been mustered into federal service, Whiteside could only take orders from Atkinson. However, Governor John Reynolds also traveled with Whiteside's men, and because neither he nor the two ranger battalions were under Atkinson's authority, Reynolds ordered Stillman's battalion forward to engage Black Hawk's band.

Whiteside told Reynolds that it was reckless to send such a small force against a numerically superior foe (for it was known that Black Hawk had as many as five hundred warriors), but despite Whiteside's protests Reynolds issued his order. Others in addition to Whiteside roundly criticized Reynolds for this negligence. One regular army officer later wrote that Reynolds "would have done for more service and less injury by remaining at his capital."[57] And while Reynolds bore the ultimate responsibility, Atkinson, had he been present with Reynolds and Whiteside and traveled with the Illinois volunteers instead of the regulars, almost certainly could have stopped Reynolds from issuing his criminally incompetent order to Stillman.

After the Battle of Stillman's Run, blood had been spilled on both sides; now there was no going back as the Indians and whites both clamored for revenge. Black Hawk was particularly incensed by the fact that he had attempted to communicate his willingness to return across the Mississippi and only had three dead warriors murdered by Stillman's men to show for his efforts. He angrily stated that "instead of this *honorable course*...I was *forced* into WAR, with about *five hundred warriors*, to contend against *three* or *four thousand*!"[58] The citizens of Illinois also screamed for war, although many expressed more fear than rage and began to abandon their isolated frontier settlements for the safety of nearby army posts. Others began to construct crude forts and blockhouses. In Washington, Andrew Jackson ordered Atkinson to "attack and disperse" the British Band.[59]

For the next several weeks, until the next major engagement at Wisconsin Heights, Black Hawk retained the initiative. This was due, in part, to the fact that the war was characterized by a series of small-scale skirmishes at which Indian warriors excelled. In fact, the regional tribes preferred small operations and hit-and-run raids to the pitched battles with definitive outcomes that characterized Euro-American warfare. Black Hawk first had his warriors plunder the supplies of food, gunpowder and ammunition left behind by Stillman's men at their camp. He then had the British Band immediately move north into present-day Wisconsin near Lake Koshkonong. This large, shallow lake, surrounded by thick, impenetrable swamps, would provide protection for his people. He laid the blame for the British Band's predicament squarely on the shoulders of Napope and his lies; nevertheless, he did not shirk from leading his warriors into battle against the armies sent against him. He vowed to avenge the deaths of his three slain warriors and told his men, "Now is the time to show your courage and bravery, and avenge the murder of our three braves!"[60]

However, for the first three weeks after Stillman's Run, the only attacks by Indians were committed by Winnebagos and Potawatomis, not the warriors of the British Band. Black Hawk managed to attract other Indians to his standard, but it was hardly the intertribal alliance for which he had hoped. Moreover, the Winnebagos and Potawatomis who joined him generally used the onset of the war as an excuse for settling old scores with white settlers. An excellent example was the small settlement along Big Indian Creek in northern Illinois. A local settler had assaulted a Potawatomi whom he found tearing down his dam. In retaliation, the Potwatomi led a fifty-man war party (which included three Sauks from the British Band) against the settlement. Twenty-three whites were present, including the man who had committed the assault. This Indian raid on May 21, 1832, came within a week of Stillman's Run, and when it was over, fifteen whites were dead. Two teenage sisters, Sylvia and Rachel Hall, were taken as prisoners and spirited to the camp of the British Band. While greatly frightened, the two girls received kind treatment from their captors. The Winnebagos later secured the sisters from the British Band and delivered them on June 1 to a settler fort at the Blue Mounds in the mining district. On the same day as the Big Indian Creek Massacre, Rock River Winnebagos attacked a fort erected by settlers on Plum River near the Mississippi. This attack was repulsed by the settlers inside, but the Winnebagos made a more successful assault three days later, on May 24, when thirteen warriors killed four white persons at Kellogg's Grove (present-day Polo, Illinois). Among the dead was Felix St. Vrain, the Sauk and Fox Indian agent.[61]

Renegade Kickapoos and Potawatomis also set fire to abandoned settler cabins along the Fox and DuPage Rivers in northern Illinois. Atkinson believed these acts were the work of the British Band, and he ordered the Illinois volunteers to scour this area. However, the loss at Stillman's Run and the news of the Big Indian Creek Massacre deflated their morale, and they demanded to be discharged from federal service. Moreover, despite their efforts, the volunteers had failed to find the British Band. They eventually found the trails that Black Hawk's followers made as they fled north to Lake Koshkonong, but the volunteers were in no mood to pursue their quarry. Instead, they conducted a final march to Ottawa, Illinois, and mustered out of federal service on May 27 and 28; thus ended the inglorious history of the first Illinois volunteer army known simply as Whiteside's Brigade. Reynolds had already called for the formation of a new army of 2,000 volunteers, but this army would not be assembled in full force until June 18. This provided Black Hawk and other Indians with designs on the Americans with additional time and virtually no military pressure. Atkinson pulled together a stronger force of regular army troops, but the tiny garrisons, which were never intended to do more than perform frontier police duties, produced only about 620 total regulars for Atkinson's army. Moreover, all were dismounted infantry, and as long as Atkinson continued to chase Indians who were mounted on horseback, he had no choice but to rely primarily on mounted militia volunteers.[62]

Meanwhile, the British Band finished its movement to Lake Koshkonong on May 28, two weeks after Stillman's Run. Black Hawk first secured provisions for his hungry followers; only when this was accomplished did his warriors begin their operations. The Indian attacks previous to this had been carried out by sympathetic Potawatomis and Winnebagos, although a few men of the British Band accompanied these war parties. Black Hawk, hearing that the first Illinois volunteer army had disbanded, believed that time was on his side. His decision to begin an active campaign was most likely spurred by the news that Atkinson and Reynolds were assembling yet another volunteer army. Black Hawk decided to have his warriors attack targets to the west, probably to draw the American forces away from the women, children and elderly members of his band at Lake Koshkonong. Black Hawk's warriors operated as two large war parties composed of roughly two hundred men each, although they worked as even smaller units when circumstances demanded it. One of these war parties committed the British Band's first known attack after Stillman's Run at a settler fort along the Apple River (near present-day Elizabeth, Illinois) on June 8, 1832, although no one on either was side was killed or even injured in this small skirmish.

One of the most significant battles during this time occurred when Dodge and twenty-nine of his men cornered eleven Sauk warriors in a horseshoe-shaped bend in the Pecatonica River. Dodge lost only two men and killed all eleven members of the Sauk war party. It was hardly a decisive battle, but it was the first real American victory of the war. Indeed, the citizens of Prairie du Chien were so impressed with this minor triumph (called the Battle of Pecatonica, or the Battle of Horseshoe Bend) that they presented Dodge with a double-barreled shotgun as a sign of their appreciation and praised Dodge for "the bold and energetic course of conduct which you have pursued in behalf of our suffering country."[63]

In fact, none of the small battles that occurred between the Battle of Stillman's Run on May 14 and the Battle of Wisconsin Heights on July 21 provided either side with any real advantage. Several of these battles (such as the First and Second Battles of Kellogg's Grove and the Battle of Apple River) were quite intense and are still remembered in the lore of the Black Hawk War, but they had no real effect on its outcome. Potawatomis and Winnebagos sympathetic to the British Band continued to commit other assaults, but these, like the attack at Big Indian Creek, generally originated in disputes with local white settlers and were even less significant in their effect on the war's course. The number of deaths on both sides was relatively minuscule but nevertheless took a definite psychological toll. John Reynolds

The Black Hawk War, April–July 1832

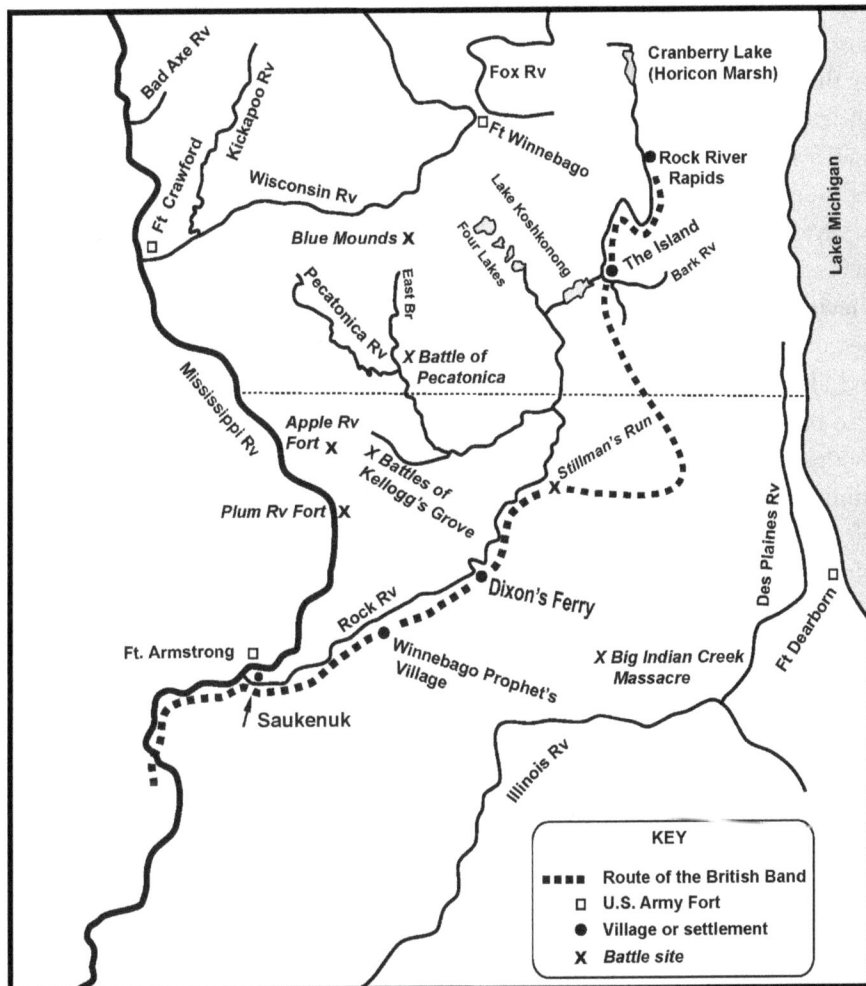

The Black Hawk War, April–July 1832. *Map produced by the author.*

summed up the effects of this phase of the war when he wrote that "blood flows here on a small scale tolerably fast."[64]

More important than these minor altercations was the creation of the second Illinois volunteer army, for it was this body of men that fought the war to a decisive and violent conclusion later in the summer. By June 18, this fresh force of Illinois volunteers consisted of three brigades. The

First Brigade, under Brigadier General Alexander Posey, had 962 men; the Second Brigade, under Brigadier General Milton K. Alexander, had 959; and the Third Brigade, the largest with 1,275 volunteers, was commanded by Brigadier General James D. Henry. Henry had served in the War of 1812 and proved to be the most talented of the three commanders. In all, Atkinson had 3,169 volunteers and 629 regular army soldiers. He bestowed on this fighting force the name the Army of the Frontier. However, the numbers of available men dwindled as the weeks went by, for Atkinson found it necessary to garrison small forts and provide guards for his logistical bases. Inevitably, soldiers also became sick and injured. Indeed, by the time he began the next phase of the war in late June 1832, Atkinson marched north to Lake Koshkonong with only about 2,100 volunteers and 450 regulars. He also had at his disposal his most fearless and aggressive commander, Henry Dodge, who by early June had about 250 volunteers he had recruited in the mining region. Of course, Dodge, like Atkinson, suffered losses for a variety of reasons, and by mid-July this number had fallen to about 150 men.[65] Nevertheless, Atkinson now had a clear numerical superiority over Black Hawk, and this would be decisive during the Battle of Wisconsin Heights.

3

Prelude to the
Battle of Wisconsin Heights

Throughout June 1832, Atkinson continued to gather intelligence on the location and future movements of the British Band as he and Reynolds organized the new army of Illinois volunteers. It was the Winnebagos and Potawatomis who ultimately provided this crucial information. Henry Dodge and Joseph Street (the Prairie du Chien Indian agent) both learned from the Winnebagos that the British Band was camped in the swamps near Lake Koshkonong; both men forwarded the information to Atkinson. The Rock River Winnebagos selected an excellent place for the British Band to make its escape after the Battle of Stillman's Run. It was an area known as "the Island" about five miles northeast of Lake Koshkonong where the Rock River (which fed into the lake) met the Bark River. It was not actually an island but was instead a piece of high ground surrounded on all sides by thick swamps. There was only one entrance into the Island from the northeast. The Island afforded Black Hawk's band excellent protection. In his autobiography, Black Hawk noted that the Island was "situate in a swampy, marshy country, (which had been selected in consequence of the great difficulty required to gain access thereto)."[66]

Military commanders and Indian agents were not the only ones who possessed knowledge of the Island. By late June, the British Band's residence there had filtered all the way down into southern Illinois. The *Sangamo Journal*, a newspaper published in Springfield, included a rough sketch of the Island in its June 28, 1832 issue. The accompanying article noted that the single route of entry (which is today traversed by Wisconsin Highway 106) made

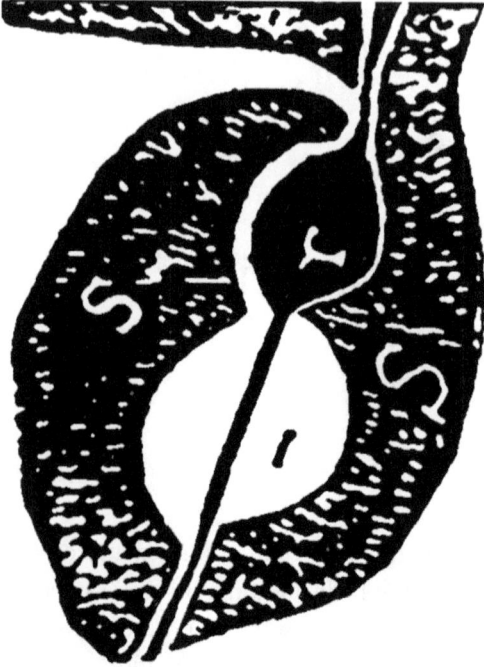

Sketch of the Island at the confluence of the Rock and Bark Rivers. The Island was the location of the first camp of the British Band at Lake Koshkonong after the Battle of Stillman's Run. The letter "s" stands for swamp lands, the letter "r" stands for the Rock River and "I" stands for the Island, the high ground where the British Band found refuge. The sketch does not accurately depict the actual terrain. *From* Sangamo Journal, *June 28, 1832.*

it an excellent defensive location. The article's author stated ominously, "Should our troops attempt to force their way over the narrow pass, they would do it at an imminent hazard."[67] It is unknown whether Atkinson ever read this short piece or spied its accompanying sketch; nevertheless, when he finally reached the Island later in July, he exercised an almost paranoid fear concerning this redoubt.

As Atkinson made his preparations, President Jackson and Secretary of War Lewis Cass grew impatient with the slow pace of the campaign and appointed Major General Winfield Scott, commander of the Eastern Department, to assemble an army of regulars from the eastern garrisons and repair to Chicago to take command of all military operations. Atkinson would not learn of this until early July 1832, well after he began his new campaign. However, Black Hawk had kept a close watch on the situation, for he sent his own warriors out as spies to track the movements and activities of the American forces. The Winnebagos also provided intelligence to Black Hawk (indeed, James D. Henry's brigade later captured two Winnebagos who confessed to being spies), and probably some sympathetic Potawatomis fed him intelligence as well, just as other members of both tribes provided information to Dodge and the regional Indian agents. From his spies, Black Hawk learned that Atkinson had a new army; it would soon march. The British Band's lack of food was becoming critical. Black Hawk's plan was to slip past Atkinson's army, flee toward the safety of the Mississippi River and return to the country of the Sauks and Foxes.[68]

On June 28, Atkinson began his march north up the Rock River from the assembly point at Dixon's Ferry. He did not move with the entire army. On June 26, he had dispatched Milton K. Alexander to take his brigade west toward the Plum River. One of Black Hawk's war parties had been active there recently, and Atkinson feared (incorrectly as it turned out) that it might be the main body of the British Band. Atkinson also ordered Alexander Posey to take his brigade to the mineral district to assist Dodge in the unlikely event that Black Hawk and his people had somehow managed to flee to this area. While Atkinson was almost certain that the British Band remained at Lake Koshkonong, he was not going to take any chances and let Black Hawk's band once again slip through his fingers. Thus, he only marched from Dixon's Ferry with Henry's brigade and his regulars; the other elements of his army, when they finished their missions, would rendezvous with him at Lake Koshkonong.

Roughly six weeks had passed since the fiasco of Stillman's Run. By this time, Brigadier General Hugh Brady had joined Atkinson. Brady was an experienced regular army officer who became one of Atkinson's most trusted subordinates. Brady took command of a portion of the Illinois volunteers, but he possessed a very low opinion of them, for they had no military training, no uniforms and virtually no discipline. He did his best to explain to Atkinson's superiors the many challenges that commanding such an army presented. In a letter to Winfield Scott, Brady specifically mentioned the "difficulties & disappointments which have been thrown in the way of General Atkinson, by the ridiculous conduct of the Militia."[69]

The volunteers' lack of discipline and inexperience became evident during the march when, on the night of July 2, a sentinel shot another volunteer thinking he might be a hostile Indian. Luckily, the man's wounds were not serious. The next day, Atkinson and his men arrived at the camp of the British Band. It had been deserted only a day or two before. It was actually the second camp of the British Band, for the first camp at the Island, while secure, offered little in the way of food. The second camp, situated closer to Lake Koshkonong, provided abundant shellfish. Indeed, piles of empty clam shells three or four feet across and a foot deep littered the ground. Needless to say, Atkinson was chagrined; he could not have the Fourth of July celebration for which he had hoped. The only Indian in the camp was an old, blind, half-starved Sauk named Kakekamak (Always Fish) who was too weak to make the journey. Atkinson questioned him about the whereabouts of the British Band. The elderly Sauk only knew that Black Hawk and his followers had moved north up the east bank of the Rock River. Later, eager to kill any Indian they could find, Posey's men murdered the defenseless Sauk.[70]

The absence of the British Band was yet another jarring reminder of Atkinson's limited abilities as a commander. He had convinced himself that the British Band would remain near Lake Koshkonong and make a final stand. Three days later, on July 6, Atkinson received a rather scathing letter from the War Department (written and sent three weeks earlier) that criticized his leadership and his inability to put an end to the insurrection. The letter stated:

> *From the instructions given, and the measures adopted by the Department...*
> *the President had a right to anticipate promptness and decision of action,*
> *and a speedy and effectual termination of Indian hostilities, and the capture,*
> *or death of Black Hawk...Some one is to blame in this matter, but upon*
> *whom it is to fall, is at present unknown to the Department.*[71]

The someone was, of course, Atkinson, and he received another dose of humiliation the next day when he learned that Winfield Scott was on his way with an army of regulars to take command of the theater of war. Atkinson became a flurry of activity and sent out many small patrols to scout the area around Lake Koshkonong in a desperate attempt to locate the British Band before Scott and his army arrived. The scouting parties confirmed what the old Sauk, Kakekamak, had told Atkinson: the British Band had fled north up the east bank of the Rock River. Atkinson, however, became wedded to a new theory that also turned out to be wrong. He believed the British Band had returned to its first camp, the Island, at the confluence of the Rock and Bark Rivers. He was lulled into this rather preposterous theory by his Winnebago guides, who were led by White Crow. As they had already done during the early weeks of the war, the Rock River Winnebagos played their duplicitous game. They seemingly expressed enthusiasm to assist Atkinson, yet at the same time they sought to render aid to the British Band. While serving as guides and scouts around Lake Koshkonong, the Winnebagos under White Crow were determined to throw Atkinson off Black Hawk's trail.

White Crow and his warriors told Atkinson that Black Hawk's camp on the Island, sitting on the opposite bank of the Bark River, had strong defenses and that it would be complete folly to attack it from the west by crossing the Rock River. Instead, White Crow and his guides urged Atkinson to ford the Bark River and attack Black Hawk's camp from the south. As part of a ruse to reinforce what was actually erroneous information, a few Winnebagos secretly crossed the Bark River on the morning of July 7 and fired on, and killed, one of Atkinson's regulars, Private David W. Dobbs.[72]

Atkinson made two attempts to storm Black Hawk's supposedly impregnable position by attempting to ford the Bark River. Throughout the day of July 7, Atkinson led elements of his army along the south bank of the river looking for a place to cross. Both banks were surrounded by thick, impenetrable swamps. The volunteers' horses often became mired in water up to their stomachs, and many threw their riders. By the end of the day, his exhausted army had marched about fifteen miles eastward, but the depth of the Bark River precluded finding a shallow place to cross. The next morning, Atkinson conferred with White Crow, who only now mentioned

Operations in the Vicinity of Lake Koshkonong, July 1832

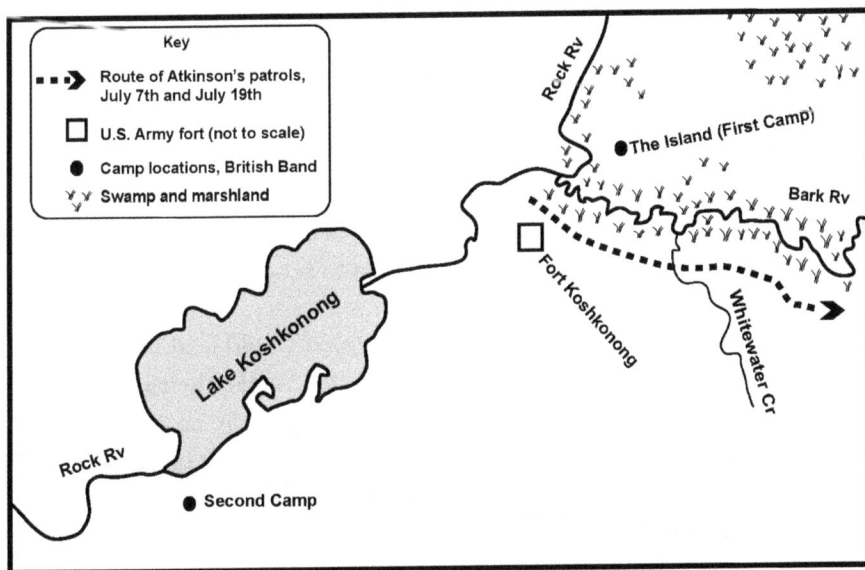

Operations in the vicinity of Lake Koshkonong, July 1832. *Map produced by the author.*

that the river afforded no places at which his horses and men could cross. Atkinson took his army back across the same ground to the place they had started the day before. The volunteers were deflated at this prospect; one of them wrote that this required him to "go back cross [sic] the worst bogs I ever crossed with a horse."[73]

On July 8, Atkinson's men arrived at the spot they had departed the previous morning. This place, at the confluence of the Bark and Rock Rivers, was directly across from Black Hawk's first camp, the Island, which, according to White Crow, was still occupied by the British Band. Atkinson decided on the morning of July 9 to construct a makeshift bridge across the Bark River at this location using sticks, logs and whatever else could be procured. The next morning, scouting parties were sent across. They brought back news that Atkinson did not want to hear: they found trails that headed farther north, but there was no sign of the British Band. Moreover, the Winnebagos named this area north of the Bark River the Trembling Lands because of the vast swamps that stretched for miles. It was as bad a place for movement as the banks of the Bark River. The absence of Black Hawk's people led Atkinson and his subordinates to the conclusion that their Winnebago guides' information had been spurious. One of the regular officers later wrote, "The Winnebagos, our professed allies, were operating on both sides and in both camps…They went out into a fog and shot a man [Dobbs]…and before the wounds of the soldier were dressed they were again in our camps, eating Uncle Sam's beef with an air of innocence."[74] Atkinson, frustrated once again, decided to cease all operations. Moreover, the men of his army were low on rations; more accurately, the volunteers were out of food. They had been issued twenty days of rations, and now, only thirteen days into the campaign, the food was depleted. Atkinson had no choice except to send the volunteers to get more rations.[75]

Little did he know at the time that this decision would lead him to Black Hawk. He ordered Dodge, Henry and Alexander to take their men to Fort Winnebago to procure supplies. Atkinson also supposedly ordered them to "pursue the trail of the enemy if it was met with in going or returning."[76] His original orders contained no such instructions. It is clear by reading his aide-de-camp's journal that these instructions were added at a later date. It appears that Atkinson later sought to take credit for ultimately finding Black Hawk. However, the historical record illustrates that he let his vanity get the best of him. His subordinate commanders and their men left on the morning of July 10. Atkinson had the regulars build a small fort, which he named Fort Koshkonong. It later became the nucleus of a settlement that would grow into a city that is today called Fort Atkinson, Wisconsin. Because of the lack of provisions, Atkinson released from service the volunteers who served in an independent scout company that was not attached to one of the three Illinois brigades. Abraham Lincoln was in this company, and he departed for New Salem, Illinois. He did not fight in any of the subsequent battles of the Black Hawk War.

Atkinson continued to send out scouting parties into the Trembling Lands in the faint hope that he might still find Black Hawk. He informed Winfield Scott that, given the fact that the British Band had fled into the vast swamps to the north, the war might conceivably continue into the winter. Scott had been busy putting together his army of regulars, which would assume the principal burden of fighting the war. By late June, Scott had about 950 men loaded on four steamboats that were scheduled to arrive at Chicago by mid-July. However, Scott's men carried more than just guns, ammunition

Sketch of Fort Dearborn at Chicago in 1830. *From* History of Jo Daviess County, Illinois, *1878.*

and their courage; they also possessed cholera. By the time the first two vessels arrived in Chicago, many men aboard had died, and their bodies had been thrown into Lake Michigan. The residents of Chicago, who shuttered themselves into Fort Dearborn in fear of an Indian attack, now fled when they heard that Scott's troops brought cholera. The other two vessels never made it to Chicago. Discipline broke down among the soldiers, and when they docked at Fort Gratiot north of Detroit, those men who were not dead or dying escaped into the surrounding countryside. Only 350 of Scott's troops who arrived at Chicago were healthy enough to fight. However, they were already too late, for by the time Scott was able to coble together these soldiers into a makeshift fighting unit and march them into battle during late July and early August 1832, the Black Hawk War was already finished.[77]

Thus, Atkinson continued to command the theater of war and concluded the conflict with the men at his disposal. Of his subordinate commanders, Henry Dodge proved to be the most valuable. The volunteers arrived at Fort Winnebago on July 11. Dodge immediately sought additional intelligence concerning Black Hawk and his followers. He was assisted in this task by the local Indian agent, John Kinzie, who provided Dodge with a party of Winnebagos and introduced Dodge to a trader of French-Winnebago ancestry named Pierre Paquette, who spoke fluent Winnebago. Paquette had relations among the Winnebagos and was well informed about all events in the tribe. He told Dodge that the British Band was still in the country of the Rock River Winnebagos and that it was camped near the Winnebago village at the Rock River Rapids (present-day Hustisford, Wisconsin). Dodge then formulated a plan to march to the Rock River Rapids in order to take the British Band by surprise. Alexander objected since they had been ordered to return immediately; thus, only Dodge and Henry participated in this ad hoc operation. Paquette and seven or eight Winnebagos from both the Rock River and Wisconsin River bands accompanied the volunteers to the Rock River Rapids. While both groups of Winnebagos were more sympathetic to Black Hawk than the United States, some were willing to assist Dodge and Henry, particularly those who had been urged to do so by the influential Paquette.[78]

The two commanders arrived at the Rock River Rapids on July 18. Dodge had about 150 men, while Henry possessed about 600. The volunteers found that the British Band was not at the Rock River Rapids, but they began to suspect that Black Hawk's people had been in the area. Like their kinsmen who had served as Atkinson's guides, the Winnebagos at the Rock River

Rapids attempted to deceive Dodge and Henry about the British Band's actual location and insisted that Black Hawk and his followers had moved north toward Cranberry Lake (present-day Horicon Marsh in Wisconsin). Dodge initially believed the Winnebagos and sent several of his men with one of Paquette's guides, a young Winnebago named Little Thunder, to convey this new intelligence. The small party had traveled only about ten or twelve miles, heading south toward Atkinson, when Little Thunder spied a trail. The trees along this path had been stripped of their bark for food. It was, indeed, the trail of the elusive British Band. Little Thunder immediately headed back to Dodge and delivered to him this valuable information on the night of July 18.[79]

Little Thunder's discovery proved to be the lucky break that Atkinson needed. Had the young Winnebago not discovered the trail, it is very likely that the British Band would have been able to escape unscathed toward the Mississippi. Black Hawk and his followers had, indeed, been hiding at the Rock River Rapids ever since they had fled Lake Koshkonong upon hearing of the approach of Atkinson and his army. Black Hawk probably decided to leave the Rock River Rapids when he learned that Dodge and Henry were approaching with more than seven hundred men. It was almost certainly the Rock River Winnebagos who alerted Black Hawk to this fact. In fact, Black Hawk and his followers probably left only a day or two ahead of the volunteers. Like Paquette, the Rock River Winnebagos were also well informed about the movements of both Indian and white forces in their country and had been since the war started.

After learning of Little Thunder's discovery, Dodge, on July 19, sent Atkinson a message with the news. At this time, Atkinson was leading his remaining soldiers in a second attempt to ford the Bark River by reconnoitering along its southern bank for a place to cross. This senseless operation was indicative of Atkinson's unimaginative nature, for he had not found any place to cross during his first attempt on July 7. Moreover, the scouting parties he sent across made it clear that the British Band was not within thirty miles of its old camp at the Island. In fact, Atkinson and his men could easily have forded the shallower Rock River at several places and avoided the deeper, swampier Bark River altogether. His insistence on continuing to execute these same ineffectual operations demonstrated not only a lack of imagination but also pure incompetence.

Upon receiving Dodge's letter of July 19, Atkinson immediately suspended his maneuvers and sent an order to Dodge and Henry to "press on with all haste and never lose sight of the object till the enemy is overtaken, defeated & if possible captured."[80] Atkinson gathered up his rump forces (which consisted of his regulars and Alexander's men) and began a march to locate the trail of the British Band. Atkinson and his forces departed the Lake Koshkonong area on July 21. However, they were already too late. Dodge and Henry had already fought and won the Battle of Wisconsin Heights.[81]

It is difficult to determine what exactly was happening in the British Band during this period. The Sauks were generally unfamiliar with the area. Black Hawk, for example, referred to Lake Koshkonong as being part of the Four Lakes chain (which is in the vicinity of present-day Madison, Wisconsin) when it is not part of this impressive string of lakes at all. The British Band's lack of familiarity with the region mattered little because they had local Winnebagos to guide them. While at Lake Koshkonong, Black Hawk's people received some corn from the Rock River Winnebagos, but they simply did not have enough food to feed an additional one thousand mouths. Black Hawk, in his autobiography, indicates that his band was critically short on food, and while he provides only the sketchiest details of the British Band's movements during the period between Stillman's Run and the Battle of Wisconsin Heights, this and other sources make it very clear that Black Hawk's followers were slowly succumbing to starvation. The news that Dodge and Henry were on their way to the Rock River Rapids, coupled with the desperate lack of food, convinced Black Hawk that he and his followers had to leave immediately and make their way to the Mississippi.

To guide his hungry followers, Black Hawk secured the services of two of the sons of the Winnebago chief Winneshiek and three other Winnebagos. Winneshiek was a member of the Mississippi River Winnebagos, but he originally hailed from the Rock River region. He was also the brother-in-law of the Winnebago Prophet and had a Sauk wife. Yet even Winnebago assistance was not enough to ensure the success of the British Band. Black Hawk and his followers had only a one- or two-day head start, but unlike the volunteers, they were hampered during their march by women, children and elderly persons. Soon, Dodge and Henry's men, who had no such burdens and now had an abundant supply of fresh provisions, would catch up with the British Band, as they could move with greater speed.[82]

On the morning of July 19, the day after they learned of Little Thunder's discovery, Dodge and Henry ordered their men to mount their horses and commence following the trail. The volunteers left their wagons behind and

The Black Hawk War, July–August 1832

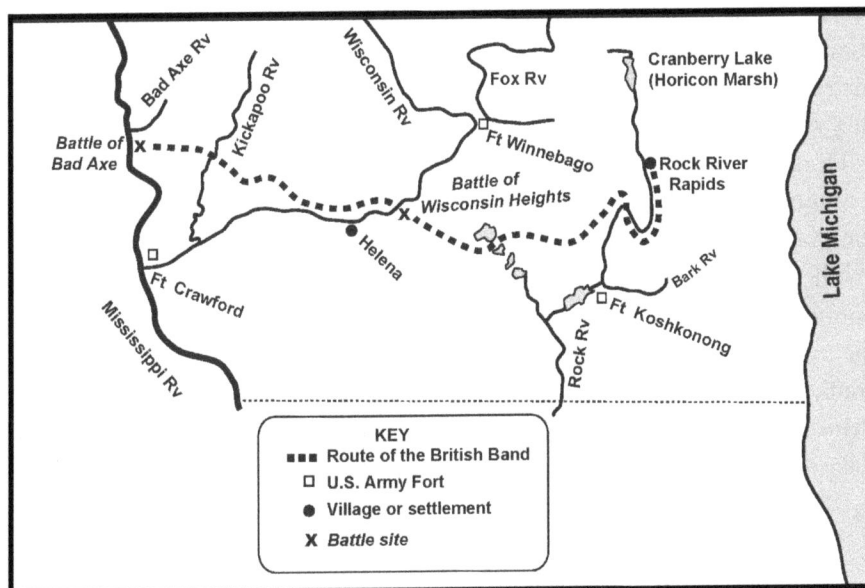

The Black Hawk War, July–August 1832. *Map produced by the author.*

took only a minimal quantity of rations so they could move quickly. Dodge and Henry pressed their men ruthlessly that morning; they wanted the volunteers to catch up to the British Band and prevent it from escaping once again. The volunteers crossed the Crawfish River (near present-day Aztalan, Wisconsin) and picked up the British Band's trail, which headed west toward the Four Lakes region. One Illinois volunteer noted that the swamps of the region continued to hamper the volunteers' movement. A few of these were so severe that the volunteers had to dismount their horses and follow them through water and mud that were often chest deep. This, one volunteer noted, allowed them to march "with great celerity."[83] The volunteers were fortunate in that the ground became increasingly less swampy and more firm as their little army pushed westward.

The volunteers made camp on the night of July 20 near present-day Rock Lake in Wisconsin. Few of the volunteers had bothered to pack their tents that morning. They began to regret this decision in the evening when it started to rain. The rain stopped during the night, but then the air turned cold. Many men did not even have blankets to guard against the chill air. The wet volunteers experienced a rather miserable night but awoke on the morning of July 20 to the familiar sound of a bugle. After a small breakfast and a chance to dry out their damp clothes, the volunteers were ready to resume their march by 7:00 a.m. Before they departed, they fired their guns to ensure they still functioned and then charged them with dry loads of gunpowder.[84]

During the course of their march, the volunteers of Henry's brigade found a Winnebago Indian whom they made a prisoner. The Indian informed the volunteers that Black Hawk's band was about two miles ahead. The Winnebago was more fortunate than other Indian prisoners taken up to that point; the volunteers simply let him go after interrogating him. Nevertheless, the intelligence he provided was undoubtedly correct, for as the volunteers continued their march, they passed several former encampments of the British Band. This meant that they were moving faster than Black Hawk's followers and gaining ground. Dodge and Henry hoped that they might catch up to Black Hawk and his followers that evening.

Dodge's battalion of about 150 men was organized into five companies, while Henry's roughly 600 men were organized as a brigade with three regiments and a scout battalion. Dodge and Henry formed their men for what looked to be an inevitable battle. The lead element consisted of Henry's scout battalion (which had two companies) commanded by Major William Ewing. Dodge posted two companies on either side of Ewing's battalion, and he posted his fifth company about one hundred yards ahead of the lead element to act as scouts. These seven companies would

Portrait of Major William Ewing. *From Frank E. Stevens,* The Black Hawk War, *1903.*

be the first into battle. This was a common tactic in early nineteenth-century warfare; the lead element served not only to scout for the enemy but also to determine its disposition by initiating and developing the battle so that the main body could move forward to finish the fight. The main body consisted of Henry's three regiments marching in column behind the lead element. Colonel Gabriel Jones's regiment was on the left, Colonel Jacob Fry's regiment was on the right and Colonel James Collins's regiment was posted in the center. The dense underbrush often made the march difficult, as did the rains, which began again and continued to dampen the morale of the volunteers. Paquette and five or six Winnebago guides continued to travel with Dodge and his men, and they remained with the volunteers until the conclusion of the Battle of Wisconsin Heights.[85]

Order of Battle for the Battle of Wisconsin Heights

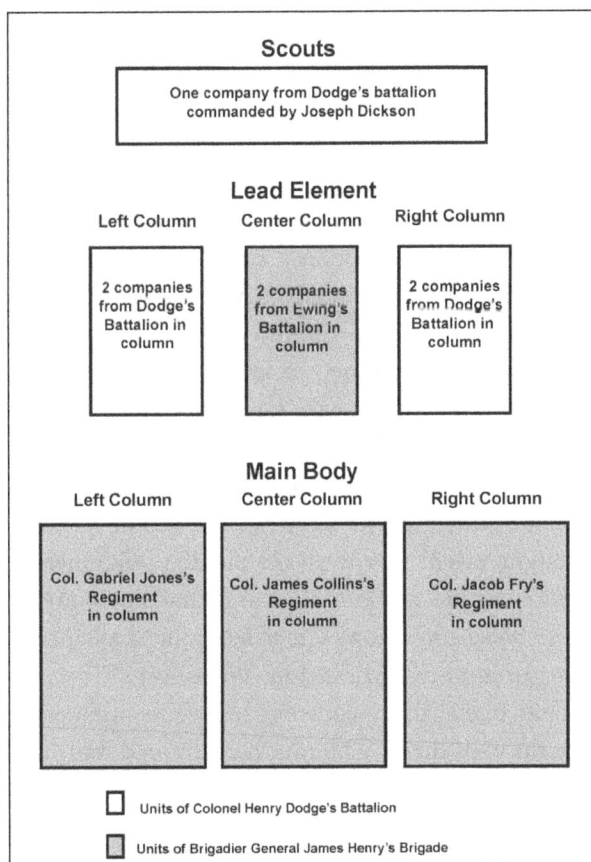

Scouts

One company from Dodge's battalion
commanded by Joseph Dickson

Lead Element

Left Column	Center Column	Right Column
2 companies from Dodge's Battalion in column	2 companies from Ewing's Battalion in column	2 companies from Dodge's Battalion in column

Main Body

Left Column	Center Column	Right Column
Col. Gabriel Jones's Regiment in column	Col. James Collins's Regiment in column	Col. Jacob Fry's Regiment in column

☐ Units of Colonel Henry Dodge's Battalion

▨ Units of Brigadier General James Henry's Brigade

Order of Battle for the Battle of Wisconsin Heights. *Diagram produced by author.*

The volunteers did not catch up with the British Band on July 20. Toward the end of the day, they reached the isthmus that stretched between the third and fourth lakes of the Four Lakes chain (Lakes Monona and Mendota, respectively). Upon reaching the northeast corner of the third lake, Henry saw a small stream that entered the lake creating a neck of land. Some of Dodge's scouts led by Captain Joseph Dickson went forward to reconnoiter the area and saw a few Indians about a mile and a half farther ahead. These warriors were the rearguard of the British Band. Upon being seen, the warriors scattered into the brush. The volunteers were closing in on Black Hawk. Paquette advised Henry and Dodge to make camp for the night, for the brush on the isthmus was thick, and even during daylight hours the movement would be difficult. It was undoubtedly a wise move, for that evening, a war party of the British Band with as many as two hundred warriors waited in an ambush position to the south.

The exact location of this position is a matter of dispute. One volunteer who served with Dodge, Daniel Parkinson, said later that it was along the Catfish River, today known as the Yahara River, which connects Lakes Monona and Mendota. This was only about a mile and a half from the volunteers' camp. Another volunteer, Charles Bracken, provided a more accurate description of the ambush site and noted that it was on the south side of Lake Mendota, about seven miles from the volunteers' position. The weight of the evidence suggests that Bracken's recollection stands as the more accurate of the two. According to Bracken, the position consisted of two pieces of high ground with a ravine running between them. Had the volunteers attempted to follow the trail that went through this ravine, they would have been easy targets for Black Hawk's warriors that evening. Dodge and Henry, heeding Paquette's counsel, decided that it was too late in the day and instead established a camp on the northeast shore of Lake Monona. Black Hawk's warriors abandoned their ambush position about midnight when they were certain the volunteers would not attack. Black Hawk's people made their camp that night about ten miles to the west, where Pheasant Branch Creek feeds into Lake Mendota on its northwestern shore (present-day Middleton, Wisconsin).[86]

That night, the volunteers settled in after eating what little food they brought with them. The rain had stopped, but they were still wet from the precipitation that had fallen earlier. Henry ordered that all the horses be tied up so that the volunteers could move out quickly the next morning.

Operations in the Vicinity of the Four Lakes July 20–21, 1832

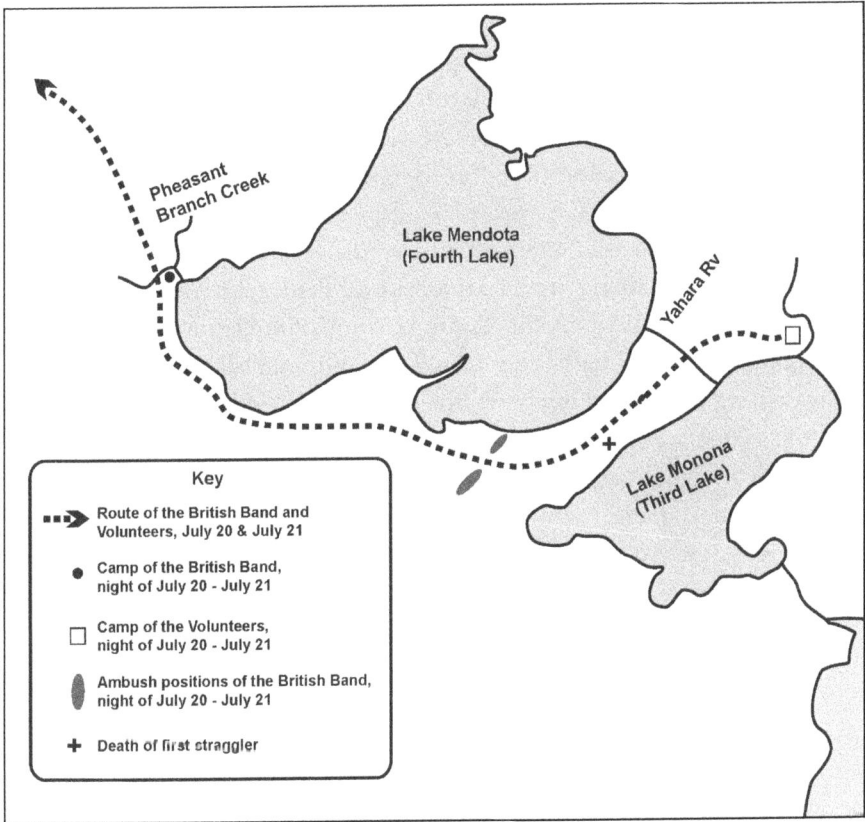

Operations in the vicinity of the Four Lakes, July 20–21, 1832. *Map produced by the author.*

After consuming their frugal dinners, the volunteers drifted off for another miserable night of sleep. Guards were posted, and they, of course, were not allowed to sleep. As the volunteers made camp that evening, Atkinson, it will be remembered, was preparing to leave Lake Koshkonong the next day and join Dodge and Henry in their pursuit of Black Hawk. However, he would be fifty miles away from the battle once it commenced at Wisconsin Heights.

Winfield Scott, who by right should have been commanding all the American military forces in the region after he arrived at Chicago on July 10, could not even leave the small hamlet. Instead, he was forced to watch helplessly as his soldiers were laid to waste by the cholera epidemic that raged among them. He did not even want the healthy troops under Atkinson to approach Chicago for fear that they, too, might become infected. Scott would be almost 150 miles from the Battle of Wisconsin Heights when it occurred, and he would not even begin his sojourn from Chicago in an effort to catch up with the rapidly moving volunteer army until eight days after the Battle of Wisconsin Heights had been fought.

Thus, the coming battle rested in the hands of Dodge and Henry, two volunteer commanders. No regular soldiers or officers of the U.S. Army would be on hand to assist them as they led their diminutive force of militia volunteers. After waking the next morning, their men would not sleep again until they had spent the entire day relentlessly pursuing their foe and fighting a pitched battle that would not end until nightfall. Despite the many discomforts the volunteers suffered, they enjoyed far better conditions than their enemy. As the volunteers slept, Black Hawk and his people spent another hellish night on the opposite side of Lake Mendota, haunted by the specter of starvation and desperately trying to make their way to the Mississippi to escape the army sent to destroy them. The next day, July 21, 1832, would be a long, hard day for both sides, but Black Hawk and his people would suffer the most.[87]

4

The Battle of
Wisconsin Heights

The morning of July 21 started the same way it always did for the volunteers: with the sound of a bugle. The volunteers rapidly consumed their breakfasts, for no time was to be lost. They readied their arms and other equipment and quickly mounted up into the order of battle they had established the day before. The temperature was seventy-one degrees Fahrenheit when they awoke; by 2:00 p.m., it would drop to sixty-eight degrees. The mild temperatures and overcast skies ensured that both the volunteers and their Indian foes would be spared the oppressively hot rays of the July sun. By 9:00 a.m., anxious to resume the march, the volunteers renewed their pursuit. Dodge's company of scouts under Captain Joseph Dickson led the tiny army. The volunteers moved out at quick time, but they soon learned that Paquette had not exaggerated when he noted the density of the underbrush on the isthmus. One volunteer later wrote:

> We soon found that the pilot [Paquette] had told us no lie; for we found the country that the enemy was leading us into, to be worse if possible, than what he had told us. We could turn neither to the right nor left, but were compelled to follow the trail the Indians had made; and that too, for a great distance at the edge of the water of the lake.[88]

For all practical purposes, the Battle of Wisconsin Heights began at the volunteers' camp on the shores of Lake Monona when they heard the shrill cry of the bugle on the morning of July 21 and awoke, groggy after a night of little sleep. As they mounted their horses and began their pursuit, they soon began to encounter stragglers of the British Band who became their first victims in what would be an ongoing battle throughout the day. Dickson's scouts spied the first straggler at about 10:00 a.m., an hour after the army had started its march. The surviving accounts all generally agree on the location: about a quarter of a mile due east of where the Wisconsin state capitol building now stands. This is roughly the present-day intersection of King and Wilson Streets. Why the Indian was there is less clear. Several sources state that he was grieving over the grave of a recently deceased relation, possibly his wife. If true, she was undoubtedly a victim of the starvation and privation that now affected all members of the British Band. Another source states that he was sick, while yet another says the straggler was hunting ducks along the shores of Lake Monona, a very unlikely scenario given the desperate escape the members of the British Band were attempting at the time. The available sources do not clearly indicate who shot the hapless Indian, but they are in complete agreement about what happened next.

Dr. Addison Philleo, a physician and newspaper editor from Galena who served as a private and surgeon under Dodge, fell upon the body of the fallen warrior, who had not yet died. He took the man's own knife and began to scalp him in the Indian manner. The pain partially revived the dying Indian, who mumbled a few incomprehensible words. Philleo taunted him by saying, "If you don't like being scalped with a dull knife, why didn't you keep a better one?"[89]

Once the volunteers had traversed the isthmus to where the state capitol now stands, they proceeded to head due west along the southern shore of Lake Mendota through what are now the grounds of the University of Wisconsin–Madison. Several of the volunteers were awestruck by the Four Lakes region. Here the country became higher and more open and presented a spectacular view of the vast expanse of Lake Mendota. One volunteer noted, somewhat dramatically, if not anachronistically (given the fact that a major metropolis now stands there), that "if those lakes [the Four Lakes] were anywhere else… they would be considered among the wonders of the world. But the country they are situated in is not fit for any civilized nation of people to inhabit."[90] Another volunteer wrote, with a bit more poetry and flourish, that

> *we followed on in pursuit passing on by the lakes which would have afforded*
> *a delightful vew* [sic] *to the traveler who was exploreing* [sic] *the country*

but we had only time to take a passing vew of the Romantic beauties of the willderness [sic] and pass on from the beautiful sandy shores of the lakes into the Broken and Barony woods.[91]

As this second observation makes clear, the volunteers could ill afford to spend their time absorbed in the breathtaking scenery, for they continued their relentless pursuit of the British Band. Because the country south of Lake Mendota was more open than it had been on the isthmus, the army picked up its pace. Now, the trail of the British Band became more evident. The volunteers even came across campfires that were only a few hours old at one spot. Given the location, it was most likely the ambush position that Black Hawk's warriors had occupied the night before.[92]

The main body of the British Band, as mentioned, had camped near the mouth of Pheasant Branch Creek, where Middleton, Wisconsin, now stands. Upon arriving at the site, the volunteers spied the fresh grave of an Indian woman, undoubtedly another victim of the starvation and exhaustion that encumbered the British Band. The volunteers then proceeded northwest toward the Wisconsin River, which was only about fifteen miles distant. The route taken by both the British Band and the volunteers roughly corresponds to present-day U.S. Highway 12 between Middleton and Sauk City, Wisconsin. The trail became increasingly easy to follow, for Black Hawk's followers had abandoned kettles, mats and other items in order lighten their load as they continued their desperate flight from the oncoming army.

By this time, Philleo had organized a special squad of ten volunteers whose mission it was to hunt down and kill any other Indian stragglers who found themselves unlucky enough to cross their path. Philleo fulfilled his duties with gusto and savagery. At some point between five and ten miles northwest of Lake Mendota, Philleo and his men spied another easy target. According to one witness, "The Indian was on foot, and a straggler, and when discovered by our advanced men, he attempted to deceive them, by crying out, Winnebago! Winnebago!"[93] Philleo and his men did not fall for the ruse, and they opened up with a volley of shots that found their mark. However, the gunfire was not immediately lethal. The mortally wounded Indian braced himself against a tree. His rifle was loaded with several balls, possibly as many as six, and he fired them at Philleo's men. At least one of the balls found its mark and lodged just below the groin and in the thigh of Isam Hardin, a member of Dodge's command from Jo Daviess County,

Illinois. The wound did not kill Hardin, at least not immediately; he died a day or two later.

The volunteers answered with a bayonet charge. The luckless Indian finally lay dead. As he had done with the first straggler, Philleo took the second Indian's scalp. For many years afterward, Philleo displayed the two scalps taken that day as war trophies at his residence in Galena. The extant accounts that describe the killing of this unfortunate warrior vary considerably in the details they provide. One volunteer stated that the Indian lingered on after the volley and tried to wrest a bayonet from one of the volunteers, who not only forced the bayonet from the Indian's hand but also ran him through with the blade until the warrior was literally pinned to earth. The enraged volunteer then proceeded to stab him seven more times. This story seems a bit fantastic, to say the least. The Indian may have been bayoneted, but such a spectacular show of strength from a dying man seems somewhat incredible, if not improbable. Some witnesses also stated that two Indians came under attack by Philleo's men during this second encounter. A few of the descriptions penned by these observers insist that this second Indian was also killed, while others say the warrior escaped. If there was a second Indian present, he almost certainly made his escape, since those sources that are the most credible only mention the death of a single Indian during the second encounter.[94]

Philleo's paper, the *Galenian*, later described his actions with an air of levity and celebration that bordered on the obscene. The editor pro tem, who managed the newspaper during Philleo's absence, wrote:

We have heard from a number of gentlemen who were in the late battle with the Indians, that the Editor *of this paper was fortunate enough to kill and* scalp *two Indians before the engagement commenced in the evening. It appears that he went in advance of the army some distance, for about half a day, in close pursuit of three Indians until he got them in a good position for attack. He then asked for five men to assist in killing them—this request was doubly granted by Gen. Dodge, who sent to his aid ten men. They continued to pursue them—the Editor in advance—who came within 20 paces of the hindmost Indian and shot him through the body, the ball entering immediately under the heart. By one of the informants, who was close at hand when the Editor shot and scalped his Indians, we received the* scalps, *sent us! Our informants state that after the first Indian had received the contents of the Editor's short gun, (a ball and three buckshot) he staggered back a few paces, leaned against a tree, levelled his piece, fired and wounded one of our men before he fell, although the lead had passed entirely through his body!...It is uncommon for Editors to fight with weapons more potent than the goose quill!—and when they do, it is the duty of the press...to note them.*[95]

This brand of savagery, while seemingly incomprehensible, nevertheless opens up a window that allows for a contemporary examination of the nature of Indian-white warfare in early America that exposes the martial customs and practices of both cultures. Indians, for example, scalped their defeated enemies, but as the events of the Black Hawk War make clear, whites often did this as well. The difference was that scalping was deeply rooted in the Indians' cultural practices. War in American Indian communities was largely an individual affair whereby warriors demonstrated their martial ardor and courage. It was the primary means by which men gained social prestige. Indeed, this was one reason that private wars were so common among the Indians of northeastern North America. When one warrior emerged victorious over another, he had the honor of taking the scalp of the man he bested, and often this man was not even dead and would be scalped alive. However, this also conferred a certain degree of prestige on the victim, for Indians believed that the defeated warrior's manhood was transferred to his opponent through the taking of the scalp. So important was this idea that

Sketch of an Indian with a scalp lock. *From George Catlin*, Letters and Notes on the Manners, Customs, Condition of the North American Indians, *1841.*

Indian warriors often wore a single long lock of hair atop their heads called a scalp lock that made it easier for an enemy to take their scalp if they were defeated in battle. The scalp lock sat atop a warrior's head as something of a dare to an enemy to try to take it.

There were several instances during the war where Black Hawk's warriors and their Winnebago and Potawatomi allies took the scalps of those they killed, both Indian and white. For example, Black Hawk's warriors scalped the fallen members of Stillman's battalion after the first battle of the war. The Potwatomis who participated in the Big Indian Creek Massacre scalped their white victims as well, and the Winnebagos who committed assaults during the war did the same. Indians who assisted the United States also scalped their Indian foes; this included a small number of Santee Sioux, Menominees and Winnebagos who served under one of Dodge's subordinates and who scalped the dead Sauks after the conclusion of the Battle of Pecatonica.[96]

Whites like Philleo, on several occasions during the Black Hawk War, also took the scalps of Indians they killed, although this was not rooted in the Euro-American way of war. Instead, it was done partially in retaliation for the scalping of whites by Indians, but it also illustrated what white Americans sought to accomplish during Indian wars. Indian hating was an American frontier tradition that stretched all the way back to Jamestown and Plymouth. Frontiersmen, who saw Indians as competitors for land and resources at best and potential enemies at worst, viewed the native inhabitants as little more than vermin deserving of extermination. Americans on the eastern seaboard, in comparison, while they often entertained rather negative and ethnocentric views concerning America's aboriginal inhabitants, rarely had contact with Indians and thus did not feel threatened by them as did their frontier kin. Easterners viewed Indians as "noble savages" who were not threats but curiosities. The frontiersmen who served as volunteers in Atkinson's army during the summer of 1832 believed that Black Hawk and his people had to be punished for their crimes. Just as important, they had to be made examples to other Indian communities that might have the temerity to rise up and attempt to turn back the inevitable tide of American expansion. The cruelties exacted on the fallen members of the British Band thus were a means by which both of these objectives, in the minds of white frontiersmen, found expression. That is why, as they made their way to the Wisconsin River in pursuit of Black Hawk's followers, the volunteer army of Dodge and Henry had as its motto "no quarter!"[97]

The Battle of Wisconsin Heights

After killing the second straggler, the volunteers came into increasing contact with the warriors who formed the rearguard of the British Band. It was now about 3:00 p.m., and the overcast skies began to release a steady rain that cooled the summer air. Napope commanded the rearguard, which had about twenty warriors divided into two parties, which posted themselves on either side of the trail that the British Band had followed and upon which the Americans were traveling in pursuit. The rearguard performed admirably by harassing the volunteers with heavy gunfire from the hilltops where it was posted. Twice the warriors of the rearguard forced the volunteers to dismount and deploy prematurely for battle. This bought Black Hawk precious time, for while his rearguard engaged the volunteers, he was a few miles ahead supervising the crossing of the Wisconsin River by the women, children and elderly members of his band. Most of his warriors had to assist in this desperate mission. Yet Black Hawk knew the volunteer army was not far behind. He had 50 Sauk warriors at his disposal to fight the pending battle. He also had about 70 Kickapoos. He did not mention the Kickapoos in his autobiography, and why he did not remains unclear, for they are mentioned in other sources. It may have been because the Kickapoos were under the direct command of their own war chief, although Black Hawk retained overall command of the entire Indian force. The Kickapoos bore the worst losses during the battle. Thus, Black Hawk had at his disposal about 120 warriors to hold off the 750 men of Dodge and Henry.[98]

Dodge became extremely animated once it was clear that the volunteers were closing in on the British Band. He drove his companies hard, and it was everything Ewing's companies could do to keep up. The lead element that these units composed was about a half hour ahead of Henry's three regiments. The pace was so fast that the horses began to give out from fatigue. According to one volunteer, "Whenever a horse gave out, the rider would dismount, throw off his saddle and bridle, and pursue on foot, in a run, without a murmur. I think the number of horses left this day, was about forty."[99]

It was now about 5:00 p.m. The rain became steadier, and the volunteers took precautions to keep their weapons dry. The first unit to make contact with Black Hawk's warriors was Dodge's company of scouts commanded by Dickson, who maintained a lead of about 150 yards over the remainder of the lead element. As one approaches the Wisconsin River along the path taken by the British Band and the volunteers, one spies the high hills that form a long ridge system that generally runs parallel to the lowlands

Portrait of Captain Joseph Dickson. *From Frank E. Stevens,* The Black Hawk War, *1903.*

along the river bottom. Black Hawk chose one of the more prominent hills to make his stand. There are actually two hills in this location—one to the north and another to the south—with a ravine that runs between them. Dickson took his scouts at full charge into this ravine in search of Black Hawk and his followers. He followed them all the way to the lowlands along the river bottom where high, thick grass grew. However, Black Hawk's warriors were determined to hold back the volunteers long enough to allow the noncombatants of the British Band to make their difficult passage across the Wisconsin River. The warriors immediately returned fire and began to push Dickson's men back from the river bottom. Dickson did not lose any men, but he nevertheless withdrew his command from the river bottom and moved to the high ground to their rear, where Dodge and Ewing were already preparing the remainder of the men of the lead element for battle. Dodge had his and Ewing's men dismount in an open area immediately behind the high ground where the volunteers would fight. Dodge detailed every fourth man to stay with the horses. The volunteers moved westward on foot to the hilltop to their front. At the same time, Dickson's men ascended the same slope as they retreated eastward so they could join the other troops of the lead element. Once this was done, Dodge's and Ewing's men formed a solid line on the ridge. One of Dickson's scouts was heard to say of the Indians, as he made his way up the ridge, "Here they come, thick as bees."[100]

At this point, a total of roughly 250 men, all from Dodge's and Ewing's battalions, composed the entire strength of the volunteers engaged in the

Battle of Wisconsin Heights, ca. 5:00 p.m.

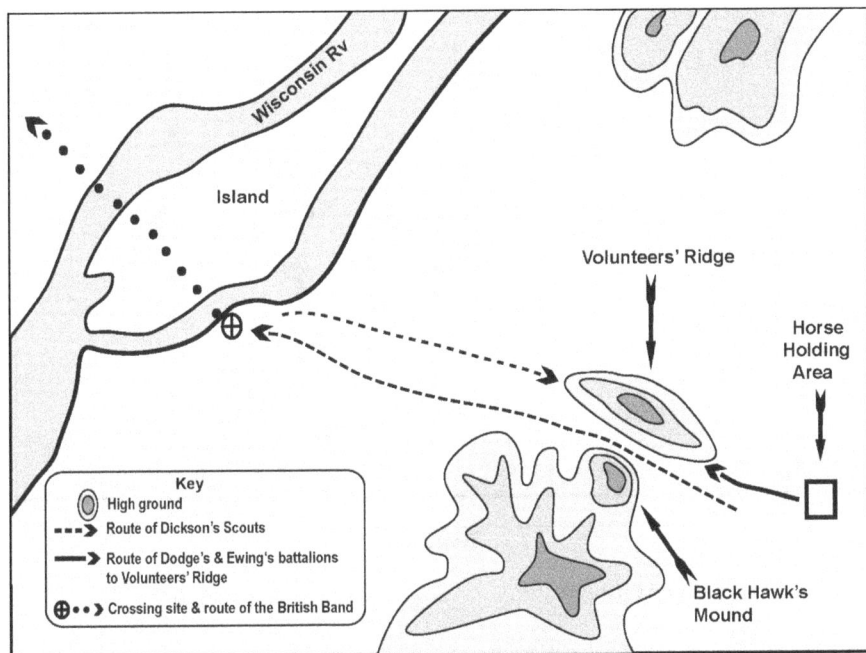

Battle of Wisconsin Heights, about 5:00 p.m. *Map produced by the author.*

fighting. Henry's three regiments would arrive shortly and greatly increase these numbers. Before that could happen, the Indian warriors made a spirited attempt to push Dodge's and Ewing's men off the ridge. Dodge ordered the volunteers to squat down so as to avoid becoming easy targets for the Indians; he readied them for the coming assault. At this point, Black Hawk's 120 warriors were outnumbered 2 to 1 but must have known that more volunteers were on the way. If they were going to force the volunteers to retreat off their ridge, now was the time to do it.

The warriors rushed at the volunteers in a direct frontal assault and let out a war cry. This was not done simply for theatrics; the war cry was done to instill fear in the enemy, and it was often quite effective. In fact, one of the reasons Stillman's men had retreated in panic five weeks earlier was because of the war cry that accompanied the assault of Black Hawk's warriors. This time, the war cry failed to yield any results. The volunteers, heeding Dodge's

Battle of Wisconsin Heights, ca. 5:00 p.m.–5:30 p.m.

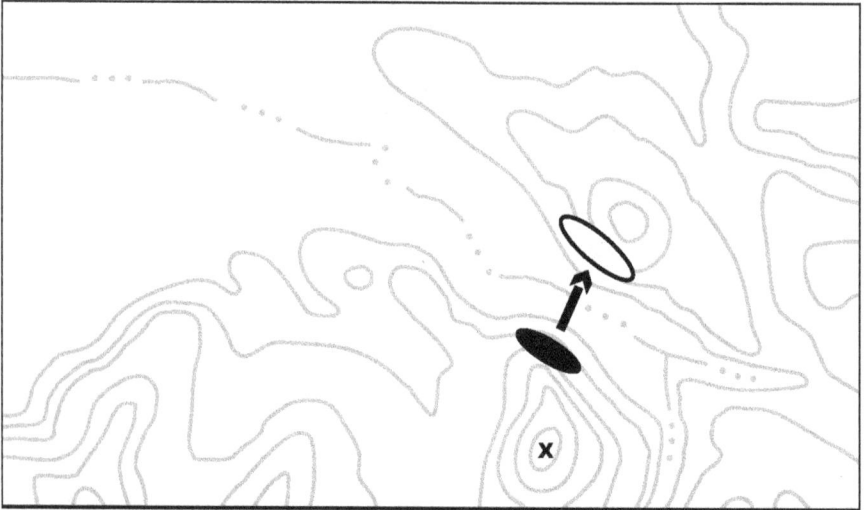

Battle of Wisconsin Heights, about 5:00– 5:30 p.m. *Map produced by the author.*

admonitions to stand fast, firmly held their ground. Dodge let the warriors (who were still mounted on their horses) get within about thirty yards of his line and then had the volunteers reply with their own war cry and a volley of shots. At least one warrior was killed and several others wounded. Clearly, this was not going to be a repeat of Stillman's Run. Seeing that their attack had failed (and probably feeling a bit unsettled by the volunteers' war whoops and the sudden volley of fire), Black Hawk's warriors broke off their attack and moved to the safety of another hilltop about two hundred yards directly to the south of the volunteers across the wide ravine. One volunteer summed up this early phase of the fighting when he wrote, "Our men then opened up a tremendous volley of musquetry upon them, and accompanied it with the most terrific yells that ever came from the head of mortals, except from the savages themselves."[101]

The Battle of Wisconsin Heights

Black Hawk at this time left the river bottom about three-quarters of a mile to the west, where his band conducted its crossing, and assumed command of his warriors. Upon arriving at the battlefield, he ascended to the summit of the hill, where his warriors had taken up their positions after their failed frontal assault. Today, this summit is still called Black Hawk's Mound. From this vantage point he had an excellent view of his own men, the volunteers on the opposing high ground and the point where his people were crossing the Wisconsin River in the distance. To add to the spectacle, he directed the battle while seated atop a white horse. He was clearly visible to the volunteers on the opposing ridgeline. Some volunteers thought he might be Napope or another, younger Sauk war leader. There is no doubt, however, that it was Black Hawk, who bolstered the courage of his fighters with a rousing speech. He later said, "I addressed them [his warriors] in a loud voice, telling them to stand their ground, and never yield it to the enemy."[102] One volunteer, realizing it was Black Hawk on the opposite hillside, later described the scene when he related:

> *An Indian of noble form stood upon a high rock, apparently engaged in cheering on his men, when a gun, considerably larger than others, was brought to bear upon him, but without effecting any injury; he soon retreated from his position. This Indian was supposed to have been the old chief Black Hawk.*[103]

Black Hawk did not retreat permanently from his position, although, as this description makes clear, he took pains to avoid being shot. Nevertheless, he clearly was in the line of fire, for his horse suffered two gunshot wounds during the course of the battle.[104]

This early phase of the Battle of Wisconsin Heights was, in many ways, the most dramatic. Two rival commanders—Henry Dodge and Black Hawk—faced off from opposing hillsides only two hundred yards apart. Both were brave, fearless and superlative leaders in combat; both were veterans of frontier warfare and had seen many battles before this one (although they had never fought on the same side). While Black Hawk retained the initiative in the early weeks of the war and had spectacular victories such as the Battle of Stillman's Run, he soon learned that in Henry Dodge he had found his match. It was in this early part of the battle that the two forces were the most evenly matched, although the volunteers had better than a two-to-one advantage in men. The tenor of the battle changed considerably when Henry arrived with his three regiments, for with their arrival, the volunteers obtained a very lopsided advantage.

Various sources provide differing estimates of time for when Henry's regiments arrived. One volunteer later noted that Henry's regiments did not arrive until about an hour after Dodge had deployed the men of the lead element on the ridgeline. Another volunteer insisted many years after the war that an hour was too long and that Henry appeared on the ridgeline with his three regiments only ten minutes after the lead element had arrived. Certainly, the excitement that came with the first volleys exchanged on the battlefield distorted the volunteers' sense of time, and thus ten minutes was probably too soon, but an hour was too long. Given these wildly differing estimates, it's safe to assume that Henry's three regiments arrived at the battlefield within about thirty minutes of the lead element. The exact time this translates into is also problematic since only a few volunteers made any mention about the hour of the day when various events transpired. One volunteer stated that the lead element's battle with the Indians began about 5:00 p.m. This is probably a relatively accurate time (or at least as accurate as the available sources will allow). Henry probably arrived with his three regiments at about 5:30 pm. Thus, the first phase of the battle between Black Hawk and Dodge lasted only about thirty minutes.[105]

Photograph of Colonel Jacob Fry. *From Frank E. Stevens,* The Black Hawk War, *1903.*

The arrival of Henry's three regiments severely limited Black Hawk's options. Dodge's and Ewing's lead element maintained the center of the formation, and the three regiments began to line up in positions on its flanks. Before this could be accomplished, Black Hawk attempted the first of two flanking maneuvers. The initial maneuver was directed against the volunteers' left wing. Henry, sensing the weakness of the left side, posted two of his regiments in this vulnerable area. Jones's regiment took up its position immediately to the left of the lead element. Collins's regiment took up position on the extreme left of the line. Black Hawk, realizing that this portion of the volunteers' line was now too strong, broke off the attack. He then attempted a second flanking maneuver and tried to do the same to the right side of the volunteers' line, but when Fry positioned his regiment to the right of the lead element, this avenue of maneuver was shut off as well. The volunteers now had the entire east–west axis of the ridgeline covered. Both of Black Hawk's attempts to dislodge the volunteers from their redoubt through flanking maneuvers had failed.

At least one volunteer believed that Black Hawk's attempt to conduct the flanking maneuver on the right side of the volunteers' line was due to his fear that Fry's men might cut him off from the main body of the British Band still conducting its crossing down at the river. This may have been so, but Black Hawk's autobiography is silent on the issue. This phase of the battle raged for about an hour and a half after Henry's regiments arrived. Not every man fought on the ridge; at least fifty—maybe more—remained in the holding area to keep watch over the hundreds of horses that carried the army to the

Battle of Wisconsin Heights, ca. 5:30 p.m.–7:00 p.m.

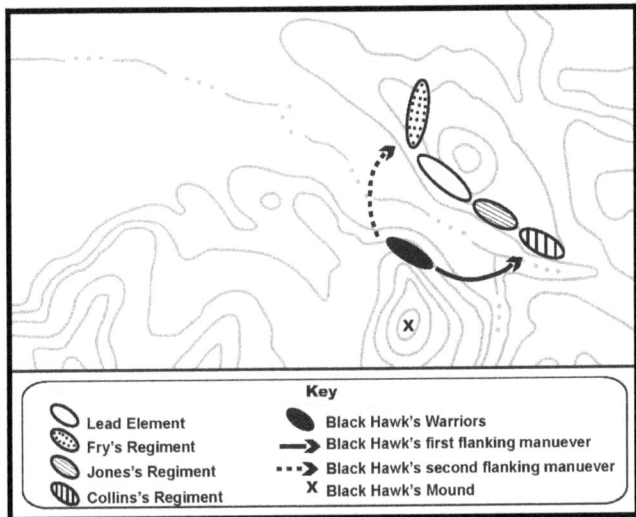

Battle of Wisconsin Heights, about 5:30–7:00 p.m. *Map produced by the author.*

Key

Lead Element
Fry's Regiment
Jones's Regiment
Collins's Regiment

Black Hawk's Warriors
Black Hawk's first flanking manuever
Black Hawk's second flanking manuever
X Black Hawk's Mound

battlefield. Nevertheless, once Henry arrived and joined Dodge, there were about 700 men on the ridge pouring a heavy volume of gunfire into Black Hawk's 120 warriors, all of whom were directly in front of the lead element just as they had been at the commencement of the battle.

Dodge continued to order the men of the volunteer army to remain under cover and to not expose themselves to the enemy's fire. They were also not to shoot unless they had a definite target. Dodge's orders were obviously effective, for only one volunteer, Thomas Jefferson Short of Jones's regiment, died that day because he continually raised his head above the fallen log behind which he had taken cover. At one point, this error proved fatal when one of Black Hawk's warriors managed to put a bullet into Short's head. The only other casualty was Jones's horse, which had been shot out from under him during the fighting (in fact, he was only one of two volunteers who had remained on their horses during the battle). Black Hawk, by his own admission, knew that the volunteers had him boxed into his position on the opposite hill. The Sauk war chief's only remaining option was to have his warriors conduct a retreat toward the Wisconsin River.[106]

At about 7:00 p.m., a decision was made for the volunteers to make a charge at Black Hawk's warriors. Who made this decision seems, initially, to be a point of dispute. Henry's men, in their reminiscences and correspondence (and Henry's own official report), state that Henry made the decision and gave the order, while Dodge's men later made contrary claims. The weight of the evidence, however, falls in

Photograph of Colonel Gabriel Jones. *From Frank E. Stevens,* The Black Hawk War, *1903.*

favor of Dodge. When the lead element first arrived at the battlefield, Dodge was clearly in charge and commanded both his men and those of Ewing. This was not surprising given the fact that Dodge held a commission as a colonel in the Michigan Territorial Militia, while Ewing's Illinois commission made him a major. Henry, on the other hand, held a commission as a brigadier general. In his report on the battle that he submitted to Atkinson, Dodge stated that he consulted with Henry on the wisdom of making a charge and that it was ultimately a joint decision and joint order, but Dodge's men later made it clear that Dodge, not Henry, was the mainspring for both the order to charge and its execution. Dodge most likely stated that it was a joint decision because he did not want to appear to be preempting a senior officer.

Regardless of such a motive, Dodge was older than Henry and more experienced in military matters generally and frontier warfare particularly. Henry had served as the sheriff of Sangamon County, Illinois, but his military résumé was far shorter than that of Dodge. The actions that led to the Battle of Wisconsin Heights, especially the detour to the Rock River Rapids, had largely been due to Dodge's initiative more so than Henry's. Even after Henry had arrived at the battlefield with his regiments, Dodge continued to act as the overall commander of the battle while Henry appears to simply have followed Dodge's lead. A final factor that solidified Dodge's leadership was the fact that both men had accepted commissions from the federal government to serve after the war in the United States Mounted Rangers, a battalion of regular soldiers mounted on horseback. This new battalion would be the predecessor to the U.S. Army Cavalry. Dodge was appointed the battalion's commander, while Henry accepted an appointment as Dodge's subordinate in the new unit. Henry's acquiescence at the Battle of Wisconsin Heights was most likely a function of the fact that he knew he would be taking orders from Dodge after the war. Thus, it was Dodge rather than Henry who was the animating force among the entire volunteer army that fought at the Battle of Wisconsin Heights. As one historian of the Black Hawk War has noted, "The Sheriff of Sangamon County was not in the same class with the Hero of Pecatonica."[107]

The charge organized by Dodge proved to the bloodiest part of the battle. Except for the single warrior (or possibly two) killed in the charge against the lead element during the early phase of the battle, it is not known how many of Black Hawk's warriors died once Henry's three regiments arrived. It was undoubtedly considerable given the fact that Black Hawk's warriors were outnumbered about six to one. Nevertheless, once Black Hawk made the decision to retreat, his warriors suffered even more casualties, if for no other reason than they had to leave those places on the ridgeline where they had found cover and concealment and move across open ground to the Wisconsin River to the place where the other members of the British Band had crossed. This exposed them to the deadly fire of the volunteers. After consulting with Henry, Dodge determined that the best tactic would be to utilize those troops on the left flank of the volunteers' line since they were in the best position to attack Black Hawk's right flank. Dodge led the assault and took all of his companies, along with those of Ewing, all of Jones's regiment and part of Collins's regiment. Dodge had the volunteers fix bayonets and move toward the high ground occupied by Black Hawk's warriors.

Battle of Wisconsin Heights, ca. 7:00 p.m.– 8:30 p.m.

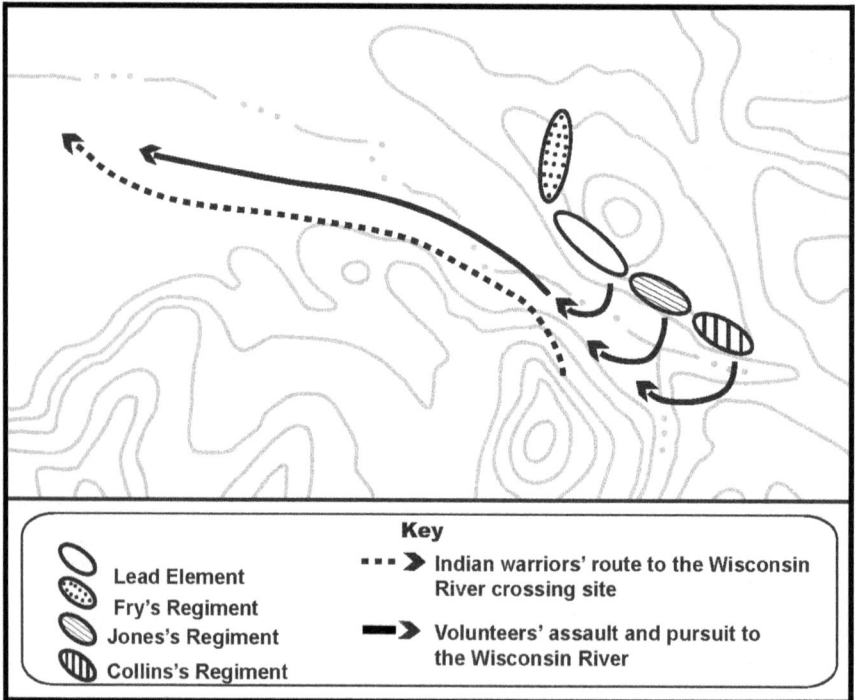

Battle of Wisconsin Heights, 7:00–8:30 p.m. *Map produced by the author.*

The Battle of Wisconsin Heights

The Indians did not stand their ground but instead started to move toward the Wisconsin River. Thus, they were essentially pursued by the charging volunteers led by Dodge. One volunteer noted that at least twenty Indians were killed at this point in the battle. This was probably a low estimate since the Indian warriors were extremely vulnerable to the volunteers' bullets as they made their way toward the Wisconsin River. Another volunteer simply noted that a "great number" of warriors were killed during the volunteers' charge, but he also had words of admiration for Black Hawk's leadership. He later wrote, "Their commander [Black Hawk]…was on a white poney [sic] on the top of a mountain in the rear of his Indians; who certainly had one of the best voices for command I ever heard. He kept up a constant yell, until his men began to retreat; when he was heard no more."[108]

The volunteers followed Black Hawk's retreating warriors all the way down to the thick grass and brush along the bottomlands of the Wisconsin River. By this time it was getting dark, and the rains that had fallen steadily for the last five or six hours continued. The wet, high grass along the river began to render the volunteers' weapons inoperative. Dodge believed the time to be about 7:00 p.m., but it was probably closer to 8:00 p.m. Dead Indian warriors littered the battlefield. It was at this point in time that Paquette and his Winnebago contingent became active. They had accompanied Dodge's command during the battle, although one volunteer noted that "the greater part of the Winnebago Indians who accompanied us…hid in sink holes or sheltered behind trees, except the White Pawnee and the son of White Crow, who together with Poquette [sic] fell into our ranks, and fought uncovered like white men."[109]

Once Black Hawk's warriors had withdrawn from the battlefield, the next battle began for the taking of scalps. According to Dodge, Paquette and his Winnebagos took eleven scalps from the dead. Satisfied with their booty, they then left the battlefield, as it was getting dark. The volunteers took another thirteen scalps. The firing stopped by the time the sun had set; Henry believed that Black Hawk's remaining warriors had taken refuge in the thick vegetation of the bottomlands but that the late hour precluded any more fighting that day. The volunteers returned to the precipice where they had fought and made camp with the expectation that they would finish off what remained of Black Hawk's fighting force in the morning. It was probably about 8:25 p.m. when the volunteers who had conducted the charge returned to the ridgeline. This is about the time that the sun sets on

July 21 at the latitude where the Battle of Wisconsin Heights took place. Soon, darkness and silence enveloped the battlefield. The only sound was that of the rain that continued to fall.[110]

The volunteers rode forty miles on horseback that day, much of it in the rain, and they fought a pitched battle at day's end. They were much fatigued and needed rest. Black Hawk's people were in far worse shape. They were still short on food and weak from hunger. In order to cross the river, they fashioned makeshift rafts by stitching together their sleeping mats and crafted crude canoes from the bark stripped from trees. Both sides expected the other to resume the attack after nightfall. However, the British Band, which had successfully managed to get its members across the Wisconsin River, was in no condition for more combat. The volunteers, on the other hand, had no means at their disposal to ford the river and continue the battle with Black Hawk's warriors. Thus, neither side resumed the fighting that evening. The volunteers ate what must have been a light dinner considering the paucity of provisions they had taken with them when they began their march earlier that morning. It was another miserable night of sleep for the volunteers. They only had three or four tents with them. The rains had soaked them thoroughly, and by 9:00 p.m., the temperature was a cool sixty-four degrees. The rain did not stop until about 11:00 p.m. that night.

The next morning, Henry and Dodge formed up the men and marched them down to where the British Band had conducted its crossing, fully expecting to find at least a few warriors ready to fight. Instead, they found only two horses that Black Hawk's followers had failed to get across the river. These would be the only "prisoners" taken by the volunteers during the Battle of Wisconsin Heights. At the crossing site, the volunteers found the trees that had been stripped by the Indians to make the crude bark canoes. They found many articles that the British Band had left behind in its haste to cross the river. They also found pools of dried blood, for Black Hawk's warriors had taken their wounded and even many of their dead off the battlefield in their desperate attempt to save as many of their comrades as possible.[111]

The number of dead on both sides was as lopsided as the battle itself. The volunteers lost only one man; they lost two if one considers the fact that Isam Hardin was shot by one of the stragglers on the march toward the Wisconsin River earlier in the day, although he did not succumb to his wounds until several days later. The volunteers also suffered eight wounded men. It was

The Battle of Wisconsin Heights

Black Hawk's warriors, however, who suffered the most horrific casualties. The warriors' position directly in front of the lead element exposed them to the heavy fire of the volunteers, particularly once Henry's regiments arrived. Far greater Indian casualties appear to have occurred once Black Hawk ordered his warriors to retreat toward the Wisconsin River. The next day, on July 22, the volunteers found dead warriors spread out on the battlefield all the way to the Wisconsin River, particularly in the thick brush and grass along the bottomlands. Initial estimates of the Indian dead by Henry and Dodge were between thirty and forty, but the number was much higher. After the Black Hawk War ended, Indian prisoners were questioned about the events at the Battle of Wisconsin Heights. One of these witnesses, a woman, put the final tally of dead warriors at sixty-eight. This number was later repeated in many sources, including the descriptions of the battle penned by white volunteers. This is undoubtedly as accurate a number as can be ascertained. Moreover, it indicates that more than half the Indian warriors who fought at the Battle of Wisconsin Heights gave their lives.[112]

However, Black Hawk's recollections stand in marked contrast to this estimate, for he noted in his autobiography that "with fifty braves, I defended and accomplished my passage over the Ouisconsin [Wisconsin River], with the loss of only SIX men…The loss of the enemy could not be ascertained by our party; but I am of opinion, that it was much greater, in proportion, than mine."[113] It is almost difficult to believe that he entertained such grossly inaccurate numbers, but with careful analysis, it is apparent that he was neither lying nor delusional. His assessment that the volunteers lost more men than he did was simply wishful thinking on his part. As far as the estimates of his own losses, these are accurate if one remembers that he did not count the Kickapoos who lost their lives. As mentioned, his force consisted of fifty Sauks and about seventy Kickapoos. Why he did not mention the Kickapoos who fought alongside his own warriors is a mystery, but there is no doubt, based on the testimony of other members of the British Band, that the Kickapoos were the very backbone of the Indian force that fought in the Battle of Wisconsin Heights. Members of the British Band stated that twelve lodges of Kickapoos were members of the band, all of which had joined Black Hawk in 1830. A lodge contained as many as twenty persons, and while some Kickapoos had abandoned the British Band by the time of the Battle of Wisconsin Heights, it is nevertheless safe to assume that at least two hundred or more remained and that roughly a quarter of them were warriors. Several members of the British Band believed that all or most of the Kickapoo warriors died in the battle; it is possible that only one of them survived.

The only estimate provided of Black Hawk's total strength during the battle was that of the Fort Winnebago sutler (a type of military general store operator) Satterlee Clark, who stated that Black Hawk had 120 men. Clark later claimed to be at the Battle of Wisconsin Heights, but his description of the battle quickly reveals this to be a bald-faced lie. He asserted that more than 3,000 volunteers participated in the battle, but volunteers who were known to be at the battle asserted that between 600 and 700 men fought under Dodge and Henry; 700 is probably closer to the truth. Despite his attempt to garnish undeserved military laurels, Clark most likely learned the details of the battle from Pierre Paquette, particularly the number of Indians who fought for the British Band. Moreover, his estimate of 120 warriors agrees with other sources. So, if Black Hawk commanded about 50 Sauk warriors, only 6 of whom died (another Sauk corroborated this number in a general sense when he stated that 5 Sauk warriors died), and other Indian witnesses asserted that all or virtually all of the Kickapoo warriors died, and another stated that a total of 68 warriors died in the battle, it's safe to assume that the vast majority of the dead warriors were Kickapoos. One member of the British Band, a thirty-year-old Fox Indian name Wa-coo-se-mok, summed up their participation when he stated tersely that "the Kickapoos fought hardest at the battle of Wisconsin."[114]

The staggering loss of the Kickapoos was just one facet of the tragedy the British Band faced at the Battle of Wisconsin Heights. Black Hawk ultimately succeeded in getting the members of his band across the Wisconsin River, but some of them continued their flight down the river in the rickety bark canoes they had fashioned. The British Band slowly began to disintegrate as a coherent, functioning entity. Black Hawk later noted:

> *Here some of my people left me, and descended the Ouisconsin* [Wisconsin River], *hoping to escape to the west side of the Mississippi, that they might return home. I had no objection to their leaving me, as my people were all in a desperate condition—being worn out with travelling, and starving from hunger.*[115]

Some of those who continued down the Wisconsin River gained the assistance of the Wisconsin River Winnebago bands. Because they were divided in their loyalties, some like White Pawnee and Little Thunder rendered assistance to the United States by serving with Paquette's detachment during the Battle of Wisconsin Heights. However, others provided better canoes to those members of the British Band fleeing down the Wisconsin River. Most of Black Hawk's followers continued to travel as a band in their nightmarish march toward the Mississippi; it was their only means and hope of returning to their own country. Because Dodge and Henry had not initially pursued them across the Wisconsin River, Black Hawk mistakenly believed that he and his people could continue unhindered in their flight. This proved to be a fateful error on Black Hawk's part, for the volunteers renewed their relentless pursuit within a week.

One person who would not travel with Black Hawk was Napope, for during the headlong rush toward the Wisconsin River on July 21, he and other members of the rearguard became separated from the main body of the British Band because of the movements of the volunteers. Napope and a companion fled to the safety of White Crow's village and remained there for six days before beginning a weeklong journey to the Mississippi, safely out of reach of the volunteer army. After crossing the Wisconsin River, Black Hawk was enraged when he learned of Napope's actions. It was the final straw in what Black Hawk saw as the lies and duplicity of the young Sauk chief, for he later noted that other members of the rearguard who also had been cut off later managed to get across the Wisconsin and rendezvous with the British Band. Black Hawk angrily noted, "I was astonished to find that Ne-a-pope [*sic*]…had not yet come in…Ne-a-pope, and one other, retired to the Winnebago village, and there remained during the war! The balance of his party, being *brave* men…returned, and joined our ranks."[116]

The volunteers remained at the battle site until July 23. The day after the battle, they dried their clothes, congratulated themselves on their great victory, built litters to transport the wounded, chatted idly and rested after two long days of riding in pursuit of the British Band. Nevertheless, Henry in particular feared that Black Hawk and his warriors might return during the night and attempt another attack. This assumption was bolstered by the fact that several men had seen smoke from a campfire across the river; it was undoubtedly one made by the British Band. That night, Henry doubled the guard, had the men sleep on their rifles and had fires built forty yards in front of the volunteers' camp. During their second night at the battle site, the volunteers had several rather eerie surprises that seemed to presage an attack. The horses were allowed to graze on a nearby pasture, but during the night they were spooked and stampeded into the camp. Then, a few hours before sunrise, the volunteers heard a haunting voice yelling from the hilltop where Black Hawk had commanded his warriors on July 21. No one could understand what was said, for it was in the Winnebago language, and Paquette and his Winnebago contingent had left the previous night. The speaker continued with his oratory for about ten or fifteen minutes. Henry and his men believed it was a signal for another attack. Henry rallied his men with a rousing speech in which he reportedly said:

> *My brave soldiers…hear your enemy on the same mountain from which you drove them only on the evening before last…there is no doubt but that they have mustered all their strength at this time: now let every mother's son be at his post…remember that you are fighting a set of demons, who have lately been taking the lives of your helpless and unoffending neighbors.*[117]

However, no attack came that night, and when men were detailed to scout the hilltop after daybreak, their mysterious night visitor had vanished. It is not known who this Indian was. Some volunteers conjectured that it was the Winnebago Prophet, which was possible. An American army officer who processed the Indian prisoners taken during the war wrote the cryptic reference "the man with a loud voice" next to the name of the Sauk warrior Ke-no-con-no-saat (He that Strikes the Foremost), which indicates that this young warrior might have been the orator. After the war, members of the British Band were asked about the event, and while none of them stated who the speaker was, they related that he addressed any Winnebagos in the camp and asked them to implore the volunteers to give up their pursuit. The orator stated that the women and children of the band were starving, that his people only wanted to cross the Mississippi in peace and that the British Band would cause no more trouble. Whoever it was may have been sent by Black Hawk (although he makes no mention of it in his autobiography), and the fact that the orator gave his address with the mistaken belief that it was translated and communicated to the volunteers may have been one of the factors that convinced Black Hawk that they would give up their pursuit of his suffering band.[118]

However, this would not come to pass. Later on the morning of July 23, the volunteers finally left the battle site. They were once again low on supplies,

The Battle of Wisconsin Heights

and the decision was made to head to the settler fort at the Blue Mounds to secure more provisions. Dodge's and Henry's men arrived that same day at the Blue Mounds after it was dark and found that part of Posey's brigade had already arrived there to help protect the small settlement. Atkinson marched from Lake Koshkonong with his regulars and Alexander's brigade. They arrived at the Blue Mounds on July 24 after a long march, the last twenty miles of which they were without water. While at the Blue Mounds, Atkinson reported the details of the battle to Scott. He mentioned that the lack of watercraft had prevented Dodge and Henry from crossing the Wisconsin River and continuing the pursuit of the British Band. Atkinson also noted that he planned to march the entire army north about twelve miles to a small lead mining settlement called Helena and cross the Wisconsin River at that point. His army was fatigued, and he knew it; he also knew that if he wanted to catch up to Black Hawk's fleeing band, he could not procrastinate. Moreover, he knew that the British Band was in far worse shape, for he told Scott, "Although we are worn down with fatigue and privation…[the enemy] must be much crippled, and is suffering for substinanc[e]."[119] He was more correct than he knew.

Thus began the next and final phase of the Black Hawk War, a phase that brought far more privation and suffering to the British Band than did the Battle of Wisconsin Heights. In retrospect, there is little doubt that the Battle of Wisconsin Heights became the definitive turning point of the Black Hawk War. Had it not occurred, Black Hawk's band would have had the ability to travel unmolested to the Mississippi River. Its members would still have suffered from a lack of food and the hardships caused by four months of constant traveling, but the death toll would not have been nearly as catastrophic. The British Band would likely have retained its organization and coherence and been able to return to the country of the Sauks and Foxes. The victory the volunteers enjoyed at the Battle of Wisconsin Heights severely weakened an already desperate band of Indians. Thus, while the final battle was still a week and a half away, it was already ordained to be the last stinging blow against a group of Indians who had lost the ability to fight and maintain a viable defense. The British Band was now susceptible, and its enemies, both Indian and white, would deliver a crushing blow that would all but eliminate what remained of Black Hawk's followers.

95

5

The Final Days of the
Black Hawk War

Atkinson and his troops arrived at Helena on July 26 and began building rafts to transport the army across the Wisconsin River. Helena was a typical lead mining settlement that had only a dozen or so log cabins, but like most of the settlements, it was deserted early in the war as its inhabitants fled to the safety of local forts and blockhouses. The abandoned cabins provided the lumber needed to produce the rafts. By the afternoon of July 28, all of the men, horses and equipment had been carried over the river, and the army resumed its march. After traveling about four miles, Atkinson's men picked up the trail of the British Band. By now, Atkinson's army, which once numbered almost four thousand, possessed a mere thirteen hundred men, of whom four hundred were regulars on foot. Atkinson had been forced to leave garrisons at his various logistics points and forts, and the inevitable losses due to sickness, injury and other such nuisances had slowly depleted his manpower.

The regulars and volunteers traveled through the unglaciated region of western Wisconsin known as the Driftless Area with high hills and towering cliffs. Several regular army officers noted that these precipices would have made excellent places for Black Hawk's warriors to harass the army as it made its way through the valleys and defiles along the trail. However, Black Hawk did not know he was being pursued; if he had, he might have attempted to slow down Atkinson's army. The British Band had almost a week's head start, but it moved slowly. The starving Indians were forced to slaughter and eat their horses. Atkinson's troops often passed by the remains of two Indian camps per day. This attested to the slow pace of Black Hawk's people. Every day after crossing the Wisconsin, the British Band had the sad task of burying its dead at each stop. The volunteers saw many dead Indians who literally had collapsed and died along the route. In one place, they came across eleven Indian graves.[120]

On August 1, Atkinson's men crossed the Kickapoo River and made camp near an open prairie. The Illinois volunteers continued their savagery, for upon finding a lone straggler, an old Sauk, they interrogated him. After he told them that the British Band was only a few miles ahead getting ready to cross the Mississippi, they immediately shot and killed the elderly Indian. He was not the only follower of Black Hawk to lose his life.

Those who fled down the Wisconsin River rather than travel overland with the main body after the Battle of Wisconsin Heights found themselves hunted as well. Captain Gustavus Loomis, the commander of Fort Crawford at Prairie du Chien, stationed a flatboat with a six-pound cannon and twenty-five regulars at the mouth of the Wisconsin River. By August 5, this small detachment had killed fifteen of Black Hawk's followers and made prisoners of another thirty-six. Joseph Street took other actions to prevent the escape of the British Band. He had his subagent, Thomas Burnett, ascend the Mississippi and visit the Winnebagos of the Mississippi River bands. Burnett convinced them to assemble at Prairie du Chien within a few days and threatened to withhold their treaty annuities if they did not. The Winnebagos, eager to stay clear of Atkinson's advancing army, readily complied. Street and Burnett were less worried about the Mississippi Winnebagos assisting Black Hawk than they were about the British Band commandeering their canoes and using them to cross the river.

By July 31, hundreds of Winnebagos in dozens of canoes had arrived at Prairie du Chien; once there, the warriors began to assist the army in rounding up those members of the British Band who fled down the Wisconsin River after the Battle of Wisconsin Heights. Loomis also hired a steamboat, the *Warrior*, to serve as an armed vessel. In addition to a six-pound cannon, the *Warrior* had a detachment of sixteen regulars. Its mission was to police the Mississippi north of Prairie du Chien and search for the British Band. Slowly, the jaws of the vice were closing around Black Hawk and his remaining followers.[121]

Loomis also sent a young lieutenant to visit the Santee Sioux at Chief Wabasha's village to warn them of the British Band's movements. The Santee

The Final Days of the Black Hawk War

Sioux were eager to attack their enemies, even if it was just the starving remnants of a renegade band. Before the young lieutenant even left the village, about 150 Santee Sioux warriors had departed to fight Black Hawk's followers. While they arrived too late to take part in the final battle, they played an important role in rounding up Black Hawk's followers afterward. This was also true of the Menominees at Green Bay. Like their allies the Santee Sioux, they were eager to engage the British Band, particularly since many of the perpetrators who massacred their kinsmen the previous summer still traveled with Black Hawk. Atkinson had actually requested their services in early July 1832, when he was at Lake Koshkonong, because he believed that the British Band might have been heading toward their country around Green Bay. By July 25, George Boyd and Samuel Stambaugh, the new and outgoing Menominee Indian agents, respectively, had organized a battalion of 232 Menominees under Stambaugh's command. The warriors served as privates, tribal war chiefs as sergeants and local fur traders as officers. Like the Santee Sioux, the Menominees missed the final battle and instead hunted down the remnants of Black Hawk's band.[122]

The *Warrior* was aptly named, for the steamboat's crew was the first to fight in what would be called the Battle of Bad Axe. On August 1, Black Hawk and his followers finally arrived at the Mississippi just south of the Bad Axe River. Only five hundred souls remained. When it first crossed the Mississippi in April, the British Band had about eleven hundred members. Roughly three hundred had been killed in the earlier battles or had died of starvation. Another three hundred or so had, since the war started in May, abandoned the British Band and found refuge among friendly Indian communities in Indiana, Illinois and Wisconsin. Black Hawk and his remaining followers gathered on the east bank of the Mississippi. Shortly after they arrived at about 4:00 p.m., they spied the *Warrior* on the river. In addition to its crew, the steamboat also possessed six citizen volunteers from Prairie du Chien eager to fight.

Black Hawk knew the captain of the *Warrior*, Joseph Throckmorton, and he was sure that he would be able spare his people further suffering by surrendering. However, Throckmorton was as keen to engage Black Hawk as everyone else on his vessel. It took Throckmorton and the others about fifteen minutes to confirm that they were, indeed, face to face with the British Band and not a group of Winnebagos. When it was clear to Black Hawk that Throckmorton and the eclectic force on board the *Warrior* were preparing to attack, he had the women and children find cover. The regulars unleashed canister shot from the cannon while the volunteers on board fired rifles and muskets. They continued to fire on the hapless Indians for the next two hours. Only one man on the *Warrior* was wounded; Black Hawk counted twenty-three dead. Throckmorton ceased the assault only when it was clear that he had to return to Prairie du Chien for more fuel. The *Warrior* would return the next day for a bloody encore.[123]

After the battle with the *Warrior*, Black Hawk announced that he was heading north to the Ojibwa country, where he had relations. About sixty of his followers, including the Winnebago Prophet, agreed to accompany him. The others opted instead to stay and cross the Mississippi. They had no idea that Atkinson's army was camped a mere ten miles to the east; had they known, more of them might have accepted Black Hawk's offer. They most likely believed that the departure of the *Warrior* gave them the respite they needed to cross the Mississippi. However, the respite would not be long enough, for Atkinson ordered his army to march at 2:00 a.m. on the fateful day of August 2.

Because Alexander's and Henry's men had let loose their horses to graze, they had to spend several hours rounding up their mounts and did not depart until after sunrise. Dodge's battalion led the march toward the Mississippi; behind him were the regulars and Posey's brigade. Dodge's scouts under Joseph Dickson had spied a trail the day before and decided to pursue it. Dickson found a small party of Indians and engaged them. He managed to kill fourteen near present-day Victory, Wisconsin. While white observers later postulated that this was a rearguard for the British Band, it was in fact Black Hawk's party. Early on the morning of August 2, a warrior who had stayed at the Mississippi caught up with Black Hawk and alerted him to the presence of Atkinson's army. Black Hawk immediately realized the gravity of the situation. His band had, indeed, been pursued after the Battle of Wisconsin Heights. He decided to return to the Mississippi. He knew that his presence would not change the outcome of the coming battle, but, he noted, "I concluded to return, and die with my people, if the Great Spirit would not give us another victory!"[124]

However, he would not get that far, for his party met with Dickson's scouts early that morning about two miles north of where the British Band was attempting to cross the river. A portion of Black Hawk's party, including Black Hawk himself, managed to hide from Dickson's scouts, but the other part of his party was not so fortunate and, as noted, lost fourteen members. While Black Hawk's party did not serve as a rearguard, it had the same effect, for upon hearing of the action, Atkinson deployed his forces. Dodge's men dismounted and stood in the center of the formation; the regulars deployed to their right; Posey lined up to the right of the regulars; and on the extreme right was Alexander's brigade. Thus, Atkinson initially had his forces moving northwest toward this initial skirmish. He soon determined that the main body of the British Band was not there but was crossing the river about two miles to the south. Dodge's men and the regulars, both on the left side of line, were able to correct their error and began to march west toward the British Band. Alexander and Posey, on the far right of the line, were unable to make the correction and marched two miles to the north toward the initial skirmish. Thus, they would be several miles from the main battle when it occurred. Their absence, however, did not change the final, grisly outcome of the Battle of Bad Axe.

Black Hawk never returned to the main body of the British Band. After his party's battle with Dickson, he and the others instead continued to make their way to the Ojibwa country. His decision did not sit well with the members of the British Band who found themselves on the east bank of the Mississippi and at the mercy of Atkinson's forces. One civil chief, Weesheet, later stated, "None of us liked the Prophet and Black Hawk leaving us as they did. We said 'now they have brought us to ruin and lost us our women and children, they have run to save their own lives.'"[125]

It was, no doubt, a rather selfish decision on Black Hawk's part not to return, and it sullied an already stained reputation that he had with his remaining followers. They now fell prey to Atkinson's army. Henry's brigade, because it had such a late start that morning, brought up the rear of Atkinson's force. Dodge and the regulars were still too far to the north when Atkinson realized his mistake, so he ordered Henry's tardy volunteers to march straight westward. By 9:00 a.m., they began to engage the actual rear guard of the British Band. Dodge and the regulars were in the best position to change the direction of their march and marched toward the battle site behind Henry's men. They soon found themselves sliding down a steep bluff toward the Indians, who were desperately attempting to find cover in the thick bottomlands of the Mississippi River.

The Indians, who had been slowly crossing the river on crude rafts since their encounter with the *Warrior* the day before, were thrown into a panic by

Battle of Bad Axe

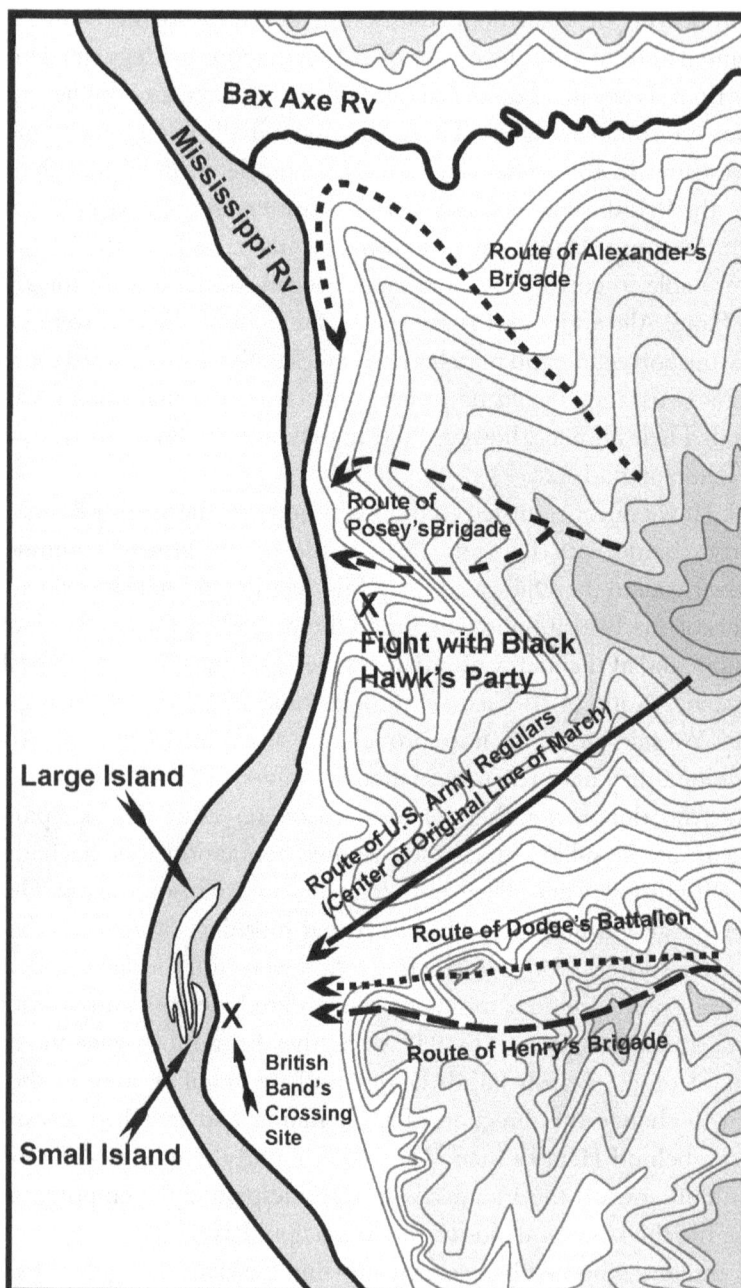

Battle of Bad Axe. *Map produced by the author.*

the arrival of Atkinson's army. The volunteers and regulars shot at anything that moved in the tall grass; often this was women and children. Soon, the members of the British Band simply began to jump into the river and attempted to take their chances swimming. There were two islands in the river at the place the Indians selected to cross. Six companies of regulars crossed a slough of waist-deep water to the larger of the two islands and flushed out the Indians who had escaped there. Many of the Indians who swam across the river might have made it had not the *Warrior* returned about noon. It now had a group of Menominee warriors who joined the vessel's crew. Those on board the *Warrior* shot at the members of the British Band swimming in the river.[126]

The battle lasted about three hours, but it is more accurately described as a massacre given the conduct of Atkinson's troops, particularly the volunteers. While some men took pains to avoid shooting women and children, it was difficult given the thick vegetation at the river bottom. However, probably more of them intentionally targeted women and children. One volunteer, after bullets grazed his hat and beard, became enraged. He saw an Indian woman with a small child on her back and yelled, "See me kill that d[am]n squaw!" and delivered a fatal wound that killed the woman and shattered the arm bone of the child.[127] The most bloodthirsty volunteer was a Dutchman named John House, or "Big Tooth John" because of his protruding eye teeth. When another volunteer refused Dickson's order to shoot an Indian child who had leaped from his hiding place, House coolly shot the boy and shortly thereafter killed another small boy who jumped up from the same spot. He even shot a small baby whose desperate mother had tied the infant to a piece of wood that she set adrift in the river in the hope of saving her child. When other volunteers reproached him for these atrocities, House merely replied, "Kill the nits, and you'll have no lice."[128] After the fighting ceased, the volunteers, as they had done before, scalped the dead Indians that littered the battlefield. Some even took strips of flesh off their backs to fashion razor straps. It was a grim and bloody finale to what was, in the end, a senseless slaughter.[129]

With the Battle of Bad Axe, the final curtain fell at the end of the last act of what had been a months-long drama, but there were several encores that had yet to be performed. The official count listed at least 150 members of the British Band dead by the end of the battle; another 40 were taken prisoner, all of whom, except one, were women and children. About 200

Indians managed to cross the river. Given these numbers, the estimate of the Indian dead was probably too low, for many bodies were later seen downriver. These were Indians who drowned or were shot while making the treacherous attempt to swim across the river. This probably accounted for another 110 people, for a total of 260 Indian dead. Atkinson lost only 15 men (one of whom died later from his wounds), and 1 Menominee warrior also died in the battle. As with the Battle of Wisconsin Heights, the numerical advantage of the American forces played a key role in determining the number of dead on both sides. In the end, a total of 77 whites died during the Black Hawk War. The British Band killed 45, and another 32 were slain by Potawatomis and Winnebagos who fought in concert with Black Hawk.[130]

The war did not end for the approximately two hundred members of the British Band who made it across the river or for those who had abandoned Black Hawk during the earlier phases of the war; they would be hunted down by their enemies: the Santee Sioux, Menominees and Mississippi River Winnebagos. On August 9 or 10, the Santee Sioux found a camp of Black Hawk's followers along the Cedar River in present-day Iowa. They launched a surprise attack at dawn that killed sixty-eight and secured another twenty-two prisoners. Only two men escaped. The Menominees under Samuel Stambaugh had similar luck when they found the trail of a small party of ten Sauks near present-day Cassville in southwestern Wisconsin. Stambaugh implored his Indian charges to simply take the entire party as prisoners, but the Menominees were too eager to avenge the killings of their people the previous year. They opened up with an incredible volume of fire that left the two men in the party dead. The remaining eight were women and children whom the Menominees made prisoners, although one child later died of wounds suffered during the attack. The firing was so heavy that one of the battalion's lieutenants received a gunshot wound to the arm from his own men. The Mississippi Winnebagos who had assembled at Prairie du Chien also assisted in killing and capturing the remaining members of the British Band; by August 22 they had secured about sixty scalps and seventy-seven prisoners.[131]

About 50 women and children and probably fewer than 10 men managed to miraculously return to their own country despite the gauntlet of Atkinson's army and the scores of Indians sent to hunt them down. Even then, because they had followed Black Hawk, Keokuk turned them over to the United States to join the other roughly 230 members of the British Band who had been taken prisoner in the days following the Battle of Bad Axe. The exact number of dead among Black Hawk's band is difficult to determine; estimates run as low as 442 and as high as 592. The average of these, about 520, is probably as close to an accurate estimate as is possible. Thus, at least half of Black Hawk's followers perished during the war, and about half of those died at the Battle of Bad Axe. Just as disheartening to Black Hawk must have been the lackluster support he received from other tribes after he crossed the Mississippi in April 1832, for only about 50 Potawatomis and 50 Rock River Winnebagos joined him, and they were more interested in avenging previous wrongs they had suffered at the hands of local white settlers than in supporting Black Hawk's scheme to remain on the east side of the Mississippi. Atkinson, on the other hand, managed to gain the support of 752 Indians who served the United States in various capacities, and this does not even include the unknown number of Mississippi River Winnebagos who hunted down what remained of the British Band after the Battle of Bad Axe.[132]

In fact, it was Mississippi River Winnebagos who delivered to federal officials the most valuable prisoner of the war: Black Hawk. After leaving his band at the Mississippi, Black Hawk made his way toward the Ojibwa country. He and his party had established a camp at the headwaters of the La Crosse and Lemonweir Rivers near present-day Tomah, Wisconsin (and not anywhere near the Wisconsin Dells as earlier histories claimed). A Winnebago named Hishoog-ka (Big Gun) stumbled across the camp and alerted the village chief at Prairie La Crosse, whose name, ironically, was also Black Hawk and who is usually called Winnebago Black Hawk to avoid confusion. The Winnebagos took Black Hawk and his party as prisoners. A young warrior named Chaashjan-ga (Wave) accompanied Black Hawk and the Winnebago Prophet to Prairie du Chien, where Chaashjan-ga delivered both men to Joseph Street and Zachary Taylor on August 27. The two fallen Indian leaders remained in the guardhouse at Fort Crawford until September 4, when they were transported down the Mississippi aboard the steamboat *Winnebago*. Also transported were Black Hawk's two sons, Nashaweskaka (Whirling Thunder) and Wathametha (Roaring Thunder).

In one of the great ironies of American history, the two army officers who accompanied Black Hawk and his fellow prisoners were Lieutenant Robert Anderson, who later defended Fort Sumter during the opening days of the Civil War, and Lieutenant Jefferson Davis, who served as the president of the Confederacy. Davis, like Satterlee Clark, later claimed to have been at the Battle of Wisconsin Heights, but Davis had been on leave for the entire duration of the Black Hawk War. His only tangible contribution was escorting the war's most famous prisoner, Black Hawk.[133]

Black Hawk made his voyage with the last members of the British Band who had been capture by the Winnebagos and Santee Sioux. These and all the other prisoners were delivered to Rock Island and turned over to Keokuk, under whose authority they now belonged. Only Black Hawk and the other prominent civil and war chiefs of the British Band remained in custody and arrived at Jefferson Barracks on September 7. While they were not mistreated in any way, they were forced to wear balls and chains to prevent escape. This was particularly humiliating to Black Hawk, for among the Indians of the Midwest, it was better for a warrior to die in battle than to live as a prisoner. In his autobiography, Black Hawk stated as much when he asserted, "A brave war chief would prefer *death* to *dishonor*...confinement, and under such circumstances, could not be less than torture!"[134]

Initially, Atkinson detained twenty of the British Band's principal leaders but released two men in mid-September 1832. Black Hawk spent the winter making pipes and otherwise passing the time with the seventeen other prominent men of the British Band. By April 1833, only six remained in confinement: Black Hawk and his son Nashaweskaka, the Winnebago Prophet and his adopted son and the civil chiefs Napope and Pamaho (Fast-Swimming Fish). On April 5, 1833—exactly one year after Black Hawk had taken the fateful step of crossing the Mississippi with his followers—Atkinson decided to send the six men to Washington, D.C., to meet the president.[135]

In addition to his fellow prisoners, Black Hawk was accompanied by a small military escort and an interpreter as he made his way first by steamboat down the Mississippi and then up the Ohio River all the way to Wheeling, Virginia, where the entire party transferred to a stagecoach. Black Hawk was astonished by the National Road along which his party traveled. He marveled at the great expenditure of labor required to build such a thoroughfare through the Appalachian Mountains. On April 22, 1833, Black Hawk and his entourage arrived in Washington, and on April 23, he had an audience with President Andrew Jackson. Both men were the same age; both had had long careers as warriors fighting on America's frontiers. Jackson demanded to know why Black Hawk had gone to war. Black Hawk showed Jackson respect, but he refused to cower or show weakness. The Winnebago Prophet spoke first and recounted the same arguments both men

The Final Days of the Black Hawk War

Portrait of President Andrew Jackson.
From Frank E. Stevens, The Black Hawk
War, *1903.*

Sketch of Black Hawk during his
incarceration wearing a cotton shirt
and blue army frock coat. *From Perry
Armstrong,* The Sauks and the Black
Hawk War, *1887.*

had stated the previous year: that Black Hawk and his followers had a right to live on the east side of the Mississippi and raise corn at the Winnebago Prophet's village. Black Hawk added a few comments when the Winnebago Prophet finished. Black Hawk hoped after this seemingly ceremonial act of contrition that he would be allowed to return home. He was shocked when Jackson told him that he and his companions were to remain as prisoners at nearby Fort Monroe, Virginia.[136]

Black Hawk's residence at Fort Monroe was much more comfortable than his earlier stay at Jefferson Barracks. In fact, he was more of a guest than a prisoner. He did not have to wear a ball and chain, but upon Jackson's orders, he doffed his Indian garb and wore instead a white cotton shirt, a silk tie and a blue army frock coat. As a sign of his determination to remain at peace and never again go to war, Black Hawk wore these clothes for the rest of his life and was even buried in them. He received many visitors, including well-known artists who painted his portrait. Black Hawk was particularly fond of the post's commander, Lieutenant Colonel Abraham Eustis, who had arrived at Chicago the previous year with Scott's forces. Jackson did not have a firm idea concerning how long Black Hawk and his companions would stay at Fort Monroe, but Secretary of War Lewis Cass, seeing that returning them to their people would not incur any significant risk, decided to end their confinement after only a month. Cass ordered that Black Hawk and his party visit Norfolk, Philadelphia, New York and Boston before returning home. The purpose of this circuitous tour was to impress Black Hawk and his companions with the size of the United States and the folly of making war against the Americans. Black Hawk's tour along America's eastern coast would achieve this goal far better than Cass could have hoped.[137]

Black Hawk and his companions departed Fort Monroe on June 4, 1833, and arrived in Norfolk later that night. Black Hawk's visit there demonstrated two elements of his eastern tour that would be repeated. First, even though it was dark when he and his small party landed, an immense crowd had formed in anticipation of his arrival. Black Hawk had no idea how the Black Hawk War had made him a celebrity throughout the United States. Second, he and his companions would continue to be awed as they saw wonders and sights they had never before seen. In Norfolk, it was the massive USS *Delaware* with its seventy-four guns at the nearby naval yard. Later, when he and his companions made an unscheduled stop in Baltimore, Black Hawk was astounded by the sheer size of the city and its seemingly limitless number of inhabitants. He stated, "On our arrival at Baltimore, we were much astonished to see so large a village; but the war chief [Black Hawk's military escort, Major John Garland] told us that we would soon see a *larger* one. This surprised us more."[138] Previously, Black Hawk had only seen small frontier hamlets such as St. Louis and Detroit. He possessed only the vaguest conceptions concerning America's thickly populated eastern coast. In Baltimore he attended the theater on the night of June 6. President Jackson was also in attendance as he made his own tour of eastern cities that summer. In Philadelphia, Black Hawk and his companions toured the national mint, the Cherry Hill Prison and the city waterworks. He was again struck by the city's size and could not believe that New York City would be even larger. Upon his arrival there, once again he and his party were thronged by massive crowds. Black Hawk had already been mesmerized by sights such as railroads and steam locomotives; he was absolutely spellbound in New York City when he witnessed a hot-air balloon float into the sky.[139]

While Boston was to be the last city on his tour, Black Hawk convinced Garland that he had seen enough and wanted to return home. Garland relented when he realized that the trip had fulfilled its purpose. He noted in a letter to Cass, "It was with difficulty they could believe their own senses" when they saw the "populous cities and the immense crowds of people, assembled in them...they had not formed even a distant conception of the extent and population of the United States."[140] That, of course, was the trip's objective: to put into the minds of Black Hawk and his companions the notion that any war against the United States was a fool's errand. Black Hawk had already sworn to remain at peace, and his eastern tour confirmed the wisdom of this decision. After a passage up the Hudson River to Buffalo, Black Hawk's party made its way through the Great Lakes to Detroit and Green Bay. By July 1833, he was once again in Prairie du Chien, and on August 3, a year and a day after the Battle of Bad Axe, he finally arrived home to the familiar Rock Island. There, he met his rival, Keokuk, under whose leadership he was now to submit. His career as a war chief was over.[141]

Black Hawk lived the rest of his days in his tribe's new home in Iowa. He built his lodge near Keokuk's village and was known to be kind to white guests when they visited. By this time, white settlers had become more numerous in the Mississippi River Valley, for Black Hawk noticed many new white settlements as he made his way to Rock Island on his voyage home in August 1833. He thought that the Mississippi was to be a permanent boundary between the two civilizations. He now learned that during his confinement, Keokuk and Wapello had agreed to sell much of eastern Iowa to the United States. Winfield Scott and John Reynolds served as federal treaty negotiators, and they demanded that the Sauks and Foxes sell about a third of their domain in Iowa as reparation for the large sums of money the United States had been forced to pay to fight the Black Hawk War. Scott and Reynolds also announced that Keokuk, although not born into a chiefly clan among the Sauks, was by President Jackson's declaration the head civil chief among the Sauks and Foxes. Keokuk's ascendancy over Black Hawk was now complete.

The treaty was signed on September 21, 1832, only a few weeks after the cessation of hostilities. The vast tract of eastern Iowa that now belonged to the United States became known as the Black Hawk Purchase. The Winnebagos fared worse, for Scott told the Winnebagos that their perfidy during the war and their support of the British Band required them to sell a significant amount of land to the United States. The Winnebago leadership, resigned to what they believed was inevitable, agreed to sell virtually all of their remaining land in southern Wisconsin to the United States on September 15, 1832.[142]

After returning to the Mississippi Valley, Black Hawk recounted his life and the events of the war to a young newspaper editor, James B. Patterson, and a Sauk and Fox interpreter named Antoine LeClaire. With Patterson's and LeClaire's assistance, Black Hawk produced one of the first authentic autobiographies of an American Indian; it is still one of the most significant sources for understanding not only the Black Hawk War but also the Battle of Wisconsin Heights. Toward the end of his biography, Black Hawk again expressed his wish that his people and white Americans should live in peace. He was true to his word, for he never again went to war. His desire to live in peace bore fruit, for on July 4, 1838, Black Hawk was the honored guest at the Independence Day celebration held by the local white settlers at the site of Fort Madison. The day must have brought back bittersweet memories. In 1809 and 1812, as a much younger man, he had joined his fellow warriors in attacks on the American fort that once stood at the same location. In 1832, his followers had gathered at the ruins of the old fort and from there took their fateful step across the Mississippi River.

Black Hawk died a few months after this celebration on October 3, 1838. The last recorded words he spoke summed up the latter years of his life. He told an assembled crowd of whites at the site of Fort Madison: "I was once a great warrior...I am now poor. Keokuk has been the cause of my present situation."[143]

Epilogue

Black Hawk's words to the crowd in July 1838 summarized the precipitous decline of his fortunes in the years after he returned from his tour of the East in 1833. One white observer in 1836 confirmed Black Hawk's deplorable status when he described him as a "poor dethroned monarch" and "an object of pity" who wore "an old frock coat and brown hat…and [carried] a cane in his hand." Along with his two sons, Black Hawk was accompanied by "his *quondam* aide-de-camp, Nah-pope [*sic*], and the prophet."[144] Yet even in the depressed circumstances in which he found himself during his later years, Black Hawk retained a bit of the spark that had made him a revered figure in his tribe many years before.

A white settler, William Smith, spied Black Hawk and other Sauks traveling on a steamboat the next year. Black Hawk still wore the frock coat he had received in Washington in 1833, and according to Smith, he spoke with "deliberation, and earnestness, evidently with a knowledge of his subject—he uses little gesticulation—and on the whole is a very respectable Indian—the whole Band appears to pay him deference even in his present Situation."[145] Reverend Cutting Marsh, a white missionary, came to a similar conclusion in 1834, when he wrote:

> [Black Hawk] *has been degraded and is not permitted to hold any office amongst his people, yet he has a very respectable band who follow him and are much attached to him…it is quite questionable whether…he is not quite as much respected as the haughty and high-minded Ke-o-kuck* [sic] *who now holds the reins of government in his own hands.*[146]

Thus, while Black Hawk may have been stripped of his authority and made a mere peon under Keokuk, his people continued to hold dear their memories of Black Hawk as the brave war chief who had once defied the might of the United States. He may not have reached the towering heights of fame or generated the hallowed memories of other great Indian leaders who preceded him, such as Tecumseh or Pontiac. Certainly, his rather selfish comportment at the Battle of Bad Axe did not endear him to many Sauks, who in the years after the war held him and his confederates, Napope and the Winnebago Prophet, responsible for the disasters that the British Band faced during the Black Hawk War of 1832. Yet despite his human faults and frailties, many Sauks must have remembered those times during Black Hawk's career when he rose above the plateau inhabited by most mortal men, and no moment in Black Hawk's life was more magnificent than his conduct at the Battle of Wisconsin Heights.

While composing his autobiography in 1833, Black Hawk provided an assessment of his leadership during the battle:

> *I would not have fought there, but to gain time for my women and children to cross…A warrior will duly appreciate the embarrassments I labored under—and whatever may be the sentiments of the* white people, *in relation to this battle, my nation, though fallen, will award to me the reputation of a great brave, in conducting it.*[147]

As Smith's and Marsh's later comments indicate, Black Hawk lived to see his vindication.

He also earned the respect of his opponents, particular U.S. Army officers who learned of his exploits from the white volunteers with whom they served. One of these was Lieutenant Philip Cooke, who served with the regulars during the Black Hawk War. While he was not at the battle, he was far more impressed with Black Hawk's accomplishments at the Wisconsin River than with those of Henry and Dodge. Cooke later wrote:

> *After all their* [the volunteers'] *boasting, the simple fact was, that Black Hawk, although encumbered with the women, children, and baggage of his whole band, covering himself by a small party, had accomplished that most difficult of military operations—to wit, the passage of a river—in the presence of three regiments of American volunteers!*[148]

Jefferson Davis, although he fabricated the story of his participation in the Battle of Wisconsin Heights, almost certainly learned, as Cooke did, the details of the battle from the volunteers. He later asserted, in elevated (if somewhat ostentatious) language:

> *This was the most brilliant exhibition of military tactics that I ever witnessed—a feat of most consummate management and bravery, in the face of an enemy of greatly superior numbers. I never read of anything that could be compared with it. Had it been performed by white men, it would have been immortalized as one of the most splendid achievements in military history.*[149]

Even if Davis was not completely honest about his service in the Black Hawk War, the former president of the Confederate States of America can at least be credited with giving credit where credit is due.

The pious platitudes of Cooke and Davis also illuminate a more fundamental, objective analysis of the Battle of Wisconsin Heights. More specifically, the massacre that the British Band suffered at the Battle of Bad Axe might very well have occurred two weeks earlier at Wisconsin Heights had Black Hawk not demonstrated the audacity to attempt a river crossing while simultaneously battling a numerically superior foe. His followers, pinned between the volunteers and the Wisconsin River, would surely have experienced a far more catastrophic loss of life on July 21 had they not conducted a crossing of the Wisconsin River. It can be argued that they suffered just that fate as they stood at the Mississippi River two weeks later, on August 2; however, this misses the point. No one knew on July 21 what lay ahead after the Battle of Wisconsin Heights. Those events were still in the unknown, indeterminate and tearful future. Had heavy rainstorms or some other obstacle slowed down Atkinson's army for just one day after Black Hawk crossed the Wisconsin River, he might just have been able to get most or even all of his suffering followers across the Mississippi before their enemies caught up with them. Also, Black Hawk and his people crossed the Wisconsin River on July 21 despite a lack of watercraft of any sort, and all but those killed in the fighting made it across or at least escaped down the river. Dodge and Henry did not even attempt to cross the Wisconsin River that night or even the next day, despite having the exact same handicaps as the British Band. Indeed, they did not cross the Wisconsin River until a week later, and even then it took Atkinson's army two days to do what the British Band accomplished in the span of a single horrific evening, while at the same time fighting a delaying action. Thus, Jefferson Davis was right to assert that had Black Hawk and his followers been white, they would have been immortalized. On reflection, he was only partially correct. Black Hawk and his followers seem to finally be receiving the admiration they rightly deserve.

As Black Hawk sat atop his white horse on the mound that still bears his name, he was only a few miles south of a spot where his people had a large village about one hundred years earlier. This place, now a city, still bears the name Prairie du Sac, or the Sauk Prairie. Directly to the south lies Sauk City, Wisconsin. By 1795, the Sauks had abandoned the area as they moved down the Wisconsin River to the Mississippi Valley. The British Band's short return to this place on July 21, 1832, was a bitter sojourn that watered the once rich soil of their ancestors with blood and tears. The location of the battlefield was in doubt for almost one hundred years, for many people who lived in the region speculated (incorrectly) that it lay directly across the river from Sauk City. One person who knew better was an Englishman named Richard Taylor, who bought a farm on the battle site in 1840. On it, he and his son found a saddle and a gun, relics left behind by either the Indians or volunteers during the Battle of Wisconsin Heights. An old volunteer who fought in the battle even visited Taylor's farm and described where both sides had fought many years earlier.

The State Historical Society of Wisconsin, with the help of Richard's son, Alfred Taylor, confirmed the location of the Battle of Wisconsin Heights in 1920. It lies just off what is today Wisconsin Highway 78, about two miles south of Sauk City. In 1923, the Daughters of the American Revolution erected a marker at the site that read simply, "Wisconsin Heights Battlefield. Near this site the Sauk chieftain Black Hawk and his band were overtaken by Wisconsin and Illinois troops on July 21, 1832. Erected by the John Bell Chapter D.A.R. Madison, September 3, 1923."[150] If the wording on the monument was neutral in its language, the speech given that day by Mrs. George S. Parker of the DAR was not. Indeed, she would have won the admiration of Henry Dodge, James D. Henry and every other volunteer who fought in the battle, for in her address Mrs. Parker "spoke briefly in defense of the pioneers and their services

Wisconsin Historical Society historical marker at the Wisconsin Heights Battle Field. *Photograph by the author.*

for civilization." The ceremony concluded with the participants singing a rousing rendition of "America."[151]

Today, the 1923 DAR ceremony seems as obnoxious in its blatantly racist sentiments as those of the volunteers who had participated in the Battle of Wisconsin Heights 91 years earlier. In 1998, the State Historical Society of Wisconsin placed a new historical marker at the location that provides a better description of the battle and the events that transpired there. It states that "because of Black Hawk's superb military strategy...approximately

700 Indians, including children and the aged, escaped down or across the Wisconsin River about one mile west of here." Thus, almost 180 years after the Battle of Wisconsin Heights, Black Hawk and his followers are finally receiving the accolades they rightly deserve. It is hoped that the ghosts of their dead that still linger over the precipices of Wisconsin Heights can now find some small measure of solace.

Notes

ABBREVIATIONS

Full bibliographic information for all sources listed below can be found in the Works Cited section. References for published works refer to page numbers or volume and page numbers. References for unpublished materials are described below in the individual entries.

A51-1833   Adjutant General's Office, Letters Received
ASP:IA   *American State Papers: Indian Affairs*
Baird MSS   Baird Papers (references are to box and folder numbers)
BHW   Whitney, *Black Hawk War*
Boilvin MSS   Boilvin Letters (references are to box, volume, and page numbers)
CWAL   Basler, *Collected Works of Abraham Lincoln*
Forsyth MSS   Forsyth Papers (references are to volume and page numbers)
HI   Wilson and Davis, *Herndon's Informants*
Ho. Doc. 2   War Department, *Annual Report, 1827*
Ho. Doc. 277   War Department, *Letter to the Secretary of War*
HOW   Smith, *History of Wisconsin*
IALT   Kappler, *Indian Affairs: Laws and Treaties*
M-1   Bureau of Indian Affairs, Microfilm Publication M-1
               (references are to reel and frame numbers)
M-21   Bureau of Indian Affairs, Microfilm Publication M-21
               (references are to reel, volume and page numbers)
M-234   Bureau of Indian Affairs, Microfilm Publication M-234
               (references are to reel and frame numbers)
M-617   Adjutant General's Office, Microfilm Publication M-617
               (references are to reel numbers)
MPHC   Holmes, et al., *Michigan Pioneer and Historical Collections*

Sen. Doc. 1	War Department, *Annual Report, 1828*
T-494	Bureau of Indian Affairs, Microfilm Publication T-494 (references are to reel and frame numbers)
TAC	Davis, *Treaties and Conventions*
Taliaferro MSS	Taliaferro Papers (reference are to volume and page numbers)
TPUS	Carter and Bloom, *Territorial Papers of the United States*
WHC	Draper, et al., *Collections of the State Historical Society of Wisconsin*
WHH	Esarey, *Messages and Letters of William Henry Harrison*

CHAPTER 1

1. Callender, "Sauk," 648; Callender, "Fox," 636.
2. Edmunds and Peyser, *Fox Wars*, 9–30, 65–77, 119–70, 198–211; Black Hawk, *Autobiography*, 47; Kay, "Fur Trade," 275–77.
3. White, *Middle Ground*, 269–314, 398–99; Tanner, *Atlas*, 54–56; Cummings, "Sauk-E-Nuk," 49–62.
4. Horsman, *Indian Policy*, 3–52, 86–97; White, *Middle Ground*, 413–74; quoted from Black Hawk, *Autobiography*, 58.
5. Wallace, *Jefferson*, 206–08, 227–28, 248–51; quoted from Dearborn to Harrison, June 27, 1804, *ASP:IA*, 1:695.
6. Wallace, *Jefferson*, 206–07, 248–51, 317; Wallace, "Prelude," *BHW*, 1:19–21; Black Hawk, *Autobiography*, 58–60.
7. Tanner, *Atlas*, 98–99; Wilkinson to Dearborn, July 22, 1805, *TPUS*, 13:168; Talks, Gaines and Sauk, June 4–7, 1831, *BHW*, 2:28; Forsyth, Original Causes, October 1, 1832, Forsyth MSS, 9:54–59; quoted from Black Hawk, *Autobiography*, 62.
8. Wallace, "Prelude," *BHW*, 1:27; Dowd, *Spirited Resistance*, 23–201; Harrison to Eustis, June 15, 1810, *WHH*, 1:427; Harrison to Eustis, August 7, 1810, *WHH*, 1:456.
9. Nichols, *Black Hawk*, 31–34; Foley, "Different Notions," 2–13; Lewis to Dearborn, July 1, 1808, *TPUS*, 14:202–03; Clark to Eustis, April 5, 1809, *TPUS*, 14:260; Harrison to Eustis, July 25, 1810, *WHH*, 1:449; Clark to Eustis, September 12, 1810, *TPUS*, 14:412–14.
10. Fiske, *American Revolution*, 173–78; Wells to Harrison, August 20, 1807, *WHH*, 1:242; Johnson to Eustis, August 7, 1810, *WHH*, 1:459; Letter to War Department, September 17, 1811, *ASP:IA*, 1:801; Forsyth to Lewis, September 7, 1812, *TPUS*, 16:264; Allen, *Indian Allies*, 54–56, 83–84, 110–15.
11. Gilpin, *War of 1812*, 3–22; Harrison to Eustis, November 18, 1811, *WHH*, 1:618–31; Rising, "Indian Depredations," 281–304; Black Hawk, *Autobiography*, 64n, 64–68; Jackson, "Old Fort Madison," 11–20, 47–62.
12. Quoted from Black Hawk, *Autobiography*, 68.
13. Stevens, "Illinois, War of 1812," 97; Horsman, "Wisconsin, War of 1812," 3–15; Taylor, "Zachary Taylor," 84–91; Allen, *Indian Allies*, 160–61; Black Hawk, *Autobiography*, 89–90.
14. Treaty of Ghent, December 24, 1814, *TAC*, 343; *Missouri Gazette and Illinois Advertiser*, July 8, 1815; July 15, 1815; *Missouri Gazette*, September 16, 1815; June

15, 1816; Fisher, "Portage des Sioux," 495–503; Treaty with Foxes, September 14, 1815, *IALT*, 121–22; Treaty with Sauks, May 13, 1816, *IALT*, 126–28; quoted from Black Hawk, *Autobiography*, 73–86, 98.

15. Jung, *Black Hawk War*, 33–36; Return of Indians, 1818–1820, *MPHC*, 23:108; Sims, "Algonkian-British," 55–91, 136–37.

16. Everhart, "Mineral Lands," 117–23; Marsh to Cass, November 20, 1826, M-1, 19:106; Kuhm, "Mining," 25–31; Forsyth to Calhoun, June 24, 1822, Forsyth MSS, 4:128–31; Forsyth to Clark, August 15, 1826, Forsyth MSS, 4:258–59; Clark to Barbour, July 11, 1827, M-234, 748:89; Boilvin to Calhoun, June 11, 1819, Boilvin MSS, 3:1:105–07; Kinzie to Cass, July 24, 1819, M-1, 6:92; Zanger, "Conflicting Concepts," 263–76; Zanger, "Red Bird," 69–70.

17. Zanger, "Red Bird," 70–72; McKenney, *Memoirs*, 127–131; Forsyth to Clark, July 9, 1827, Forsyth MSS, 4:274–76; Street to Barbour, November 15, 1827, Ho. Doc. 277, 14–15; Marsh to Clark, July 20, 1827, M-234, 748:138–40; Marsh to Cass, July 4, 1827, *TPUS*, 11:1096–97; Taliaferro to Clark, August 8, 1827, M-234, 757:20–21; Marsh to McKenney, July 10, 1827, M-234, 419:937–38; Forsyth to Clark, July 28, 1827, Forsyth MSS, 6:66; Taliaferro to Clark, August 17, 1827, Taliaferro MSS, 4:101–02.

18. Butte des Morts Treaty Journal, 1827, T-494, 2:3–4; Cass to Marsh, July 4, 1827, M-234, 748:103–04; McKenney to Barbour, August 4, 1827, M-234, 419:952; Fort Howard Post Returns, July–August 1827, M-617, 488; Fort Snelling Post Return, July 1827, M-617, 1193; Fort Armstrong Post Return, July 1827, M-617, 41; Nichols, "Jefferson Barracks," 321–22; Nichols, *Atkinson*, 116–27, 135–36; Atkinson to Gaines, September 28, 1827, Ho. Doc. 2, 156–57; McKenney to Cass, August 18, 1827, M-1, 21:61; Cass to Barbour, August 17, 1827, M-234, 419:779; Childs, "Recollections," *WHC*, 4:172–73; Ourada, *Menominee*, 83–84, 232–35.

19. McKenney, *Memoirs*, 95–100, 108–13; Atkinson to Gaines, September 17, 1827, Ho. Doc. 2, 151; Atkinson to Gaines, September 28, 1827, Ho. Doc. 2, 157–58; Nichols, *Atkinson*, 131–35.

20. Quoted from McKenney to Barbour, September 17, 1827, Ho. Doc. 277, 11.

21. Cass to Barbour, August 17, 1827, M-234, 419:780; Macomb to Porter, November 1828, Sen. Doc. 1, 26; Turner, "Fort Winnebago," *WHC*, 14:69–73.

22. Lurie, "Chaetar," 167–68; Forsyth to Cass, September 10, 1827, M-1, 21:102; Forsyth to Clark, October 15, 1827, Forsyth MSS, 6:78; Hickerson, *Chippewa*, 66, 76–90; Kurtz, "Economic and Political," 37–54; Forsyth to Clark, September 30, 1818, Forsyth MSS, 4:61–62; Forsyth to Clark, May 6, 1830, Forsyth MSS, 6:125–26; Street to Clark, September 21, 1830, M-234, 696:215; Marsh to Clark, May 30, 1827, M-234, 748:94; Stuart to Eaton, February 9, 1830, *TPUS*, 12:125–26; Messengers of Ta-oman, May 17, 1830, M-234, 749:945–46.

23. Eid, "National War," 125–37; Wallace, "Prelude," *BHW*, 1:7–9; Treaty with Sioux, etc., August 19, 1825, *IALT*, 250–55; Cass and Clark to Barbour, September 1, 1825, T-494, 1:750–51; Snelling to Atkinson, May 31, 1827, *TPUS*, 11:1082–83; Forsyth to Clark, June 15, 1827, Forsyth MSS, 4:271–72; Street to Clark, August 25, 1828, M-234, 696:97; Taliaferro, Daily Journal, January 4,

1829, Taliaferro MSS, 8:211; Clark to Eaton, August 18, 1829, M-234, 749:726–27; Forsyth to Clark, May 6, 1830, Forsyth MSS, 6:126; Hagan, *Sac and Fox*, 116.

24. Street to Clark, February 2, 1831, M-234, 749:1151; Street to Cass, July 12, 1831, M-234, 696:355; Schoolcraft to Cass, July 17, 1831, M-234, 420:691–92; Stambaugh to Cass, August 16, 1831, M-234, 315:527–29; Street to Loomis, July 31, 1831, *BHW*, 2:114–15.

25. Hall, *Uncommon Defense*, 99–100; quoted from Cass to Clark, August 25, 1831, M-21, 7:7:338.

CHAPTER 2

26. Forsyth to Clark, May 24, 1828, Forsyth MSS, 6:81–82; Forsyth to Clark, June 10, 1828, Forsyth MSS, 6:83–85; Stevens, *Black Hawk War*, 77–79; Black Hawk, *Autobiography*, 110–12; Wallace, "Prelude," *BHW*, 1:29–30; quoted from Forsyth to Clark, May 17, 1829, Forsyth MSS, 6:97–99.

27. Forsyth to Clark, May 17, 1829, Forsyth MSS, 6:97–99; quoted from Journal of Prairie du Chien Treaty, 1829, T-494, 2:193.

28. Nichols, *Black Hawk*, 78–85; Hagan, *Sac and Fox*, 94–96; Turner, *Red Men*, xiv–xv.

29. Callender, "Great Lakes-Riverine," 616–20; Michelson, Notes, 1; Jones, *Ethnography*, 82–84; Skinner, *Observations*, 27; Wallace, "Prelude," *BHW*, 1:4–9; Black Hawk, *Autobiography*, 52–53, 81–83, 93; Metcalf, "Who Should Rule," 659–61; Clark to Eaton, January 17, 1831, M-234, 749:1126.

30. Black Hawk, *Autobiography*, 113–37; *Niles Weekly Register*, May 4, 1833; Atwater, *Remarks*, 65, 90, 134; Clark to Secretary of War, August 12, 1831, *BHW*, 2:136; Forsyth to Clark, August 7, 1827, Forsyth MSS, 6:71–72; Forsyth to Clark, June 10, 1828, Forsyth MSS, 6T:83–85; Forsyth to Clark, June 22, 1828, Forsyth MSS, 6:88–89; Treaty of Ghent, December 24, 1814, *TAC*, 343.

31. Black Hawk, *Autobiography*, 113–20; Dunlap, Sale of Lands, 2–3; St. Vrain to Clark, April 6, 1832, *BHW*, 2:231; Wallace, "Prelude," *BHW*, 1:46; Forsyth to Clark, May 25, 1830, Forsyth MSS, 6:132; Gibson, *Kickapoos*, 80–87; Examination of Prisoners, August 19, 1832, *BHW*, 2:1028; Kay, "Fur Trade," 275.

32. St. Vrain to Clark, May 15, 1831, *BHW*, 2:7–8, 8n; Street to Eaton, July 12, 1831, M-234, 696:355; Reynolds to Jackson, August 2, 1831, *BHW*, 2:122n; Clark to Cass, August 12, 1831, *BHW*, 2:135–37; Reynolds to Clark, May 26, 1831, *BHW*, 2:13; Clark to Gaines, May 28, 1831, *BHW*, 2:16–17; Reynolds, *My Own Times*, 208; Gaines to Reynolds, May 29, 1831, *BHW*, 2:22–23; Gaines to Jones, June 14, 1831, *BHW*, 2:48; Jefferson Barracks Post Returns, May–June 1831, M-617, 545; Gaines to Jones, May 30, 1831, *BHW*, 2:25–26.

33. Quoted from Black Hawk, *Autobiography*, 124, 136–37.

34. McCall to McCall, June 17, 1831, *BHW*, 2:55–57; Talks, Gaines and Sauk, June 4–7, 1831, *BHW*, 2:27–29; quoted from Black Hawk, *Autobiography*, 124–27.

35. Talks, Gaines and Sauk, June 4–7, 1831, *BHW*, 2:27–31; Gaines to Jones, June 8, 1831, *BHW*, 2:36.

36. Deposition of Pennington, October 24, 1831, *BHW*, 2:172; Gaines to unknown, June 20, 1831, *BHW*, 2:63; quoted from Black Hawk, *Autobiography*, 127–28.

37. Reynolds, *My Own Times*, 211–15; Reynolds to Edwards, June 18, 1831, *BHW*, 2:59; Letter from Rushville, June 20, 1831, *BHW*, 2:64–66, 71n; Gaines to unknown, June 2, 1831, *BHW*, 2:63; McCall to McCall, June 23, 1831, *BHW*, 2:74–75; Fort Armstrong Post Return, June 1831, M-617, 41; McCall to McCall, July 1, 1831, *BHW*, 2:90–93.
38. Gaines to White, July 6, 1831, *BHW*, 2:102–03; McCall to McCall, July 1, 1831, *BHW*, 2:92–93; Staff Officer to unknown, July 1, 1831, *BHW*, 2:93–95; Quaife, *Early Day*, 44–48; Return of Pike's Company, June 16–July 2, 1832, *BHW*, 1:113–15; quoted from Black Hawk, *Autobiography*, 128–29.
39. Hagan, *Sac and Fox*, 132.
40. Articles of Agreement, June 30, 1831, *BHW*, 2:85–88; quoted from McCall to McCall, July 5, 1831, *BHW*, 2:98.
41. Hagan, *Sac and Fox*, 132–34.
42. Nichols, *Black Hawk*, 100; Journal of a Council, September 5, 1831, *BHW*, 2:155–59; Wallace, "Prelude," *BHW*, 1:40–47; Answer of Black Hawk, April 26, 1832, *BHW*, 2:312–13; Examination of Prisoners, August 20, 1832, *BHW*, 2:1034–35; quoted from Black Hawk, *Autobiography*, 130–33, 140.
43. Black Hawk, *Autobiography*, 133–35; Clark to Cass, December 6, 1831, *BHW*, 2:205–06; Kinzie to Cass, March 1, 1832, M-234, 696:402–03; Atkinson to Macomb, April 3, 1832, *BHW*, 2:224; Atkinson, Orders, April 5, 1832, *BHW*, 2:225–26; Thian, *Notes*, 107; Silver, *Gaines*, 132, 146, 160–61; Nichols, *Atkinson*, 3–68, 169–75; Eby, *Disgraceful Affair*, 29–30.
44. St. Vrain to Clark, April 6, 1832, *BHW*, 2:230–31; Black Hawk, *Autobiography*, 124–25, 136; Matson, *Memories*, 105–06; Forsyth, Original Causes, October 1, 1832, Forsyth MSS, 9:54–59; Bliss to Atkinson, April 9–12, 1832, *BHW*, 2:237–39; Hughes to Atkinson, April 13, 1832, *BHW*, 2:248.
45. Examination of Prisoners, August 27, 1832, *BHW*, 2:1056–57; Stambaugh to Boyd, August 13, 1832, *BHW*, 2:1074; Smith to Atkinson, April 13, 1832, *BHW*, 2:249; Dixon to Stillman, April 28, 1832, *BHW*, 2:325; Matson, *Memories*, 105; Black Hawk, *Autobiography*, 136–37, 136n, 146; Davenport to Atkinson, April 13, 1832, *BHW*, 2:247; Wallace, "Prelude," *BHW*, 1:39–40; Bliss to Atkinson, April 9–12, 1832, *BHW*, 2:237–39.
46. Nichols, *Atkinson*, 158; quoted from Atkinson to Reynolds, April 13, 1832, *BHW*, 2:245–46.
47. Atkinson to Dodge, April 14, 1832, *BHW*, 2:255–56; Atkinson to Gratiot, April 15, 1832, *BHW*, 2:257; Atkinson to Macomb, April 19, 1832, *BHW*, 2:278; St. Vrain to Clark, April 18, 1832, *BHW*, 2:277; Gratiot, Journal, 16–22 April, *BHW*, 2:1302–03.
48. Quoted from Black Hawk, *Autobiography*, 138–39.
49. Talks, Atkinson, Whirling Thunder, White Crow, April 28, 1832, *BHW*, 2:321–23; Examination of Prisoners, August 19, 1832, *BHW*, 2:1028–33; Jung, *Black Hawk War*, 78–79, 177–78.
50. Reynolds to Atkinson, April 16, 1832, *BHW*, 2:263; Reynolds, Orders, April 20, 1832, *BHW*, 2:284–85; quoted from Lincoln, Speech, July 27, 1848, *CWAL*, 1:509–10.

51. Young, et al., to Reynolds, April 20, 1832, *BHW*, 2:288–89; Reynolds, Orders, April 23, 1832, *BHW*, 2:298–99; Return of Whiteside's Brigade, April 16–May 28, 1832, *BHW*, 1:123–24; Atkinson to Dodge, April 25, 1832, *BHW*, 2: 304–05; Pelzer, *Dodge*, 8–54, 67; Jung, *Black Hawk War*, 72, 101–03.
52. Quoted from Gratiot to Atkinson, April 27, 1832, *BHW*, 2:317–18; and from Black Hawk, *Autobiography*, 138–39.
53. Quoted from St. Vrain to Clark, April 18, 1832, *BHW*, 2:277.
54. Quoted from Irwin to Herndon, September 22, 1866, *HI*, 353.
55. Clary to Herndon, October 1866, *HI*, 372; quoted from Greene to Herndon, May 30, 1865, *HI*, 18–19.
56. Black Hawk, *Autobiography*, 137–45; Wakefield, *History*, 45–47; Militia Officer's Report, May 18, 1832, *BHW*, 2:387–88; Stillman to *Missouri Republican*, June 19, 1832, *BHW*, 2:635–36; Examination of Prisoners, August 20, 1832, *BHW*, 2:1034; Trask, *Black Hawk*, 183–86; Jung, *Black Hawk War*, 88–89.
57. Atkinson to Macomb, May 10, 1832, *BHW*, 2:362; Hagan, "Atkinson and Militia," 194–97; Whiteside to Atkinson, May 18, 1832, *BHW*, 2:386–87; quoted from [Backus], "Brief History," *MPHC*, 12:426.
58. Hauberg, "Black Hawk War," 118; quoted from Black Hawk, *Autobiography*, 144–46.
59. War News from Galena, May 16, 1832, *BHW*, 2:377; Owen to Stuart, May 21, 1832, *BHW*, 2:399–400; quoted from Macomb to Atkinson, May 22, 1832, *BHW*, 2:409.
60. Starkey, *Warfare*, 17–56; Street to Atkinson, June 6, 1832, *BHW*, 2:536–38; quoted from Black Hawk, *Autobiography*, 137, 144–53.
61. Matson, *Memories*, 117–27, 149–53; Statement of Munson, October 10–11, 1834, *BHW*, 2:1287–1292, 1293n; Black Hawk, *Autobiography*, 147, 151–53; Examination of Prisoners, August 27, 1832, *BHW*, 2:1055; Wacker to Atkinson, January 17, 1833, M-234, 728:316; La Salle County Circuit Court Order, May 21, 1834, *BHW*, 2:1283; Clifton, *Prairie People*, 233; War News from Galena, May 30, 1832, *BHW*, 2:488–89; Anderson, Memoranda, August 27, 1832, *BHW*, 2:1057.
62. Owen to Hogan and Huston, May 24, 1832, *BHW*, 2:431–32; Atkinson to Johnson, May 20, 1832, *BHW*, 2:395; Atkinson to Macomb, May 30, 1832, *BHW*, 2:478; Atkinson to Macomb, May 23, 1832, *BHW*, 2:412; Atkinson to Macomb, May 25, 1832, *BHW*, 2:435; Johnston, Journal, May 19–May 29, 1832, *BHW*, 2:1311–13, 1311n–12n; Taylor to Atkinson, May 26, 1832, *BHW*, 2:453; quoted from Orr to Sawyer, July 1, 1832, *BHW*, 2:726; Reynolds, *My Own Times*, 235–39; Return of U.S. Army Troops, August 3, 1832, *BHW*, 1:576–77.
63. Statement of Munson, October 10–11, 1834, *BHW*, 2:1288–89; Black Hawk, *Autobiography*, 143–49; Porter's Grove Council, June 3–4, 1832, *BHW*, 2:511–13; Strode to Atkinson, June 10, 1832, *BHW*, 2:566; Iles, *Sketches*, 49; Eby, *Disgraceful Affair*, 183; Sherman to Dodge, May 30, 1832, *BHW*, 2:487; Dodge to Sherman, June 16, 1832, *BHW*, 2:607–08; Gehon to Sherman, June 17, 1832, *BHW*, 2:614; quoted from Citizens of Prairie du Chien to Dodge, July 3, 1832, *BHW*, 2:737.
64. Jung, *Black Hawk War*, 106–23; quoted from Reynolds to Edwards, June 22, 1832, *BHW*, 2:649.

65. Reynolds, *My Own Times*, 244–45; Stevens, "Forgotten Hero," 77–94; Return of Illinois Mounted Volunteers, June 1832, *BHW*, 1:572–73; Return of U.S. Army Troops, August 2, 1832, *BHW*, 1:576–77; Atkinson to Jones, November 19, 1832, *BHW*, 2:1209; Atkinson to Scott, July 9, 1832, *BHW*, 2:753; Illinois Companies Attached to Michigan Territory Volunteers, May–September 1832, *BHW*, 1:526–33; Bracken, "Further Strictures," *WHC*, 2:404; Dodge to Atkinson, July 18, 1832, *BHW*, 2:820.

CHAPTER 3

66. Porter's Grove Council, June 4, 1832, *BHW*, 2:511, 513n; Street to Atkinson, June 6, 1832, *BHW*, 2:536; Atkinson to Taylor, June 7, 1832, *BHW*, 2:538; Atkinson to Macomb, June 15, 1832, *BHW*, 2:589; Robb to Atkinson, June 12, 1832, *BHW*, 2:580–81; Cass to Scott, June 15, 1832, *BHW*, 2:590–93; quoted from Black Hawk, *Autobiography*, 146–47, 153–54.

67. Quoted from *Sangamo Journal*, June 28, 1832.

68. Street to Atkinson, June 6, 1832, *BHW*, 2:536; Atkinson to Taylor, June 7, 1832, *BHW*, 2:538; Atkinson to Macomb, June 15, 1832, *BHW*, 2:589; Robb to Atkinson, June 12, 1832, *BHW*, 2:580–81; Cass to Scott, June 15, 1832, *BHW*, 2:590–93; Reynolds, *My Own Times*, 255–59; Black Hawk, *Autobiography*, 147, 150, 153–54.

69. Atkinson to Jones, November 19, 1832, *BHW*, 2:1209; Atkinson to Posey, June 28, 1832, *BHW*, 2:696–98; quoted from Brady to Scott, June 26, 1832, *BHW*, 2:685.

70. Atkinson to Jones, November 19, 1832, *BHW*, 2:1209; Johnston, Journal, June 28–July 3, 1832, *BHW*, 2:1315–16; Wakefield, *History*, 76–81; Ogden, "Narrative," 42.

71. Atkinson to Cass, July 6–7, 1832, *BHW*, 2:742–43; quoted from Robb to Atkinson, June 12, 1832, *BHW*, 2:580–81.

72. Atkinson to Cass, July 6–7, 1832, *BHW*, 2:743; Wakefield, *History*, 80; Johnston, Journal, July 3–19, 1832, *BHW*, 2:1316–18; Gratiot, Journal, July 5–15, 1832, *BHW*, 2:1304; Parkinson, "Notes," *WHC*, 10:206–07; Justice, Journal, *BHW*, 2:1323; Thayer, *Hunting a Shadow*, 352, 410–11.

73. Johnston, Journal, July 7–8, 1832, *BHW*, 2:1317; Atkinson to Jones, November 19, 1832, *BHW*, 2:1210; Wakefield, *History*, 81–83; quoted from Shaw, Journal, July 8, 1832, *BHW*, 2:1334.

74. Atkinson to Dodge, July 8, 1832, *BHW*, 2:751; Johnston, Journal, July 8–9, 1832, *BHW*, 2:1317; Atkinson to Jones, November 19, 1832, *BHW*, 2:1210; Wakefield, *History*, 81–84; Armstrong, *Sauks*, 443; quoted from [Backus], "Brief History," *MPHC*, 12:434.

75. [Backus], "Brief History," *MPHC*, 12:430, 434; Johnston, Journal, July 9–10, 1832, *BHW*, 2:1317.

76. Quoted from Johnston, Journal, July 9, 1832, *BHW*, 2:1317.

77. Atkinson, Orders, July 9, 1832, *BHW*, 2:754; Atkinson, Orders, July 10, 1832, *BHW*, 2:758; Johnston, Journal, July 9–13, 1832, *BHW*, 2:1317–18, 1317n; Atkinson to Jones, November 19, 1832, *BHW*, 2:1210; Mayne, "Old Fort,"

197–201; Suppinger, "Private Lincoln," 48–49; Atkinson to Scott, July 11, 1832, *BHW*, 2:763; Jung, *Black Hawk War*, 139–41.

78. Dodge to Atkinson, July 14, 1832, *BHW*, 2:791; Zanger, "Pierre Paquette," 298–303; De La Ronde, "Narrative," *WHC*, 7:350; Decorah, "Narrative," *WHC*, 13:453; Hagan, "Dodge-Henry," 381.

79. Hagan, "Dodge-Henry," 381–83; Parkinson, "Strictures," *WHC*, 2:393; Bracken, "Further Strictures," *WHC*, 2:402–07; Dodge to Atkinson, July 18, 1832, *BHW*, 2:820; Wakefield, *History*, 103–06.

80. Jung, *Black Hawk War*, 146, 234n; Dodge to Atkinson, July 19, 1832, *BHW*, 2:825–84; Johnston, Journal, July 14–21, 1832, *BHW*, 2:1318; Atkinson to Scott, July 17, 1832, *BHW*, 2:814; Cooke, *Scenes and Adventures*, 168–69; quoted from Atkinson to Henry and Dodge, July 20, 1832, *BHW*, 2:832.

81. Atkinson to Scott, July 21, 1832, *BHW*, 2:839–40; Johnston, Journal, July 20–21, 1832, *BHW*, 2:1318.

82. Black Hawk, *Autobiography*, 147, 153–54; Examination of Prisoners, August 19, 1832, *BHW*, 2:1028–33; Examination of Prisoners, August 20, 1832, *BHW*, 2:1034–35; Street to Atkinson, August 13, 1832, *BHW*, 2:998; Council, Atkinson and Winnebagos and Menominee, August 6, 1832, *BHW*, 2:951; Porter's Grove Council, June 4, 1832, *BHW*, 2:510; Bracken, "Narrative," *HOW*, 219.

83. Bracken, "Narrative," *HOW*, 219; Parkinson, "Pioneer," *WHC*, 2:355–56; quoted from Wakefield, *History*, 106.

84. Wakefield, *History*, 106–07; Justice, Journal, *BHW*, 2:1324.

85. Justice, Journal, *BHW*, 2:1324; Wakefield, *History*, 103, 107–08; Dodge to Atkinson, July 18, 1832, *BHW*, 2:820; Bracken, "Further Strictures," *WHC*, 2:412; Dickson, "Narrative," *WHC*, 5:316; Bracken, "Narrative," *HOW*, 220; Magoon, "Memoirs," 431; *General Regulations for the Army*, 124; Parkinson, "Pioneer," *WHC*, 2:358; Parkinson, "Notes," *WHC*, 10:207; Bracken, "Further Strictures," *WHC*, 2:407.

86. Wakefield, *History*, 106–08; Bracken, "Further Strictures," *WHC*, 2:408; Justice, Journal, *BHW*, 2:1324. For the position of the ambush site, see Parkinson, "Pioneer, *WHC*, 2:355–56; Parkinson, "Notes," *WHC*, 10:207; Bracken, "Narrative," *HOW*, 219–20.

87. Wakefield, *History*, 106–08; Atkinson to Scott, July 21, 1832, *BHW*, 2:839–40; Johnston, Journal, July 20–21, 1832, *BHW*, 2:1318; Scott to Cass, June 11–12, 1832, *BHW*, 2:767–70; Scott to Atkinson, June 12, 1832, *BHW*, 2:778–79; Scott to Atkinson, August 1, 1832, *BHW*, 2:910; Black Hawk, *Autobiography*, 155.

CHAPTER 4

88. Henry to Atkinson, July 23, 1832, *BHW*, 2:858; Thayer, *Battle of Wisconsin Heights*, 107; Bracken, "Further Strictures," *WHC*, 2:408; quoted from Wakefield, *History*, 108.

89. Parkinson, "Strictures," *WHC*, 2:395; Parkinson, "Notes," *WHC*, 10:210; Parkinson, "Pioneer," *WHC*, 2:356; Chapman, "Early Events," *WHC*, 4:345; Wakefield, *History*, 109; Bracken, "Further Strictures," *WHC*, 2:408; Company

of Stephenson, September 14, 1832, *BHW*, 1:532; quoted from Magoon, "Memoirs," 431.

90. Parkinson, "Notes," *WHC*, 10:208; Henry to Atkinson, July 23, 1832, *BHW*, 2:858; quoted from Wakefield, *History*, 109.

91. Quoted from Justice, Journal, *BHW*, 2:1324.

92. Magoon, "Memoirs," 431.

93. Ibid., 431; Parkinson, "Pioneer," *WHC*, 2:356–57; Barton, "Retreat," 61–67; Wakefield, *History*, 110; quoted from Parkinson, "Notes," *WHC*, 10:208.

94. Parkinson, "Pioneer," *WHC*, 2:356–57; Wakefield, *History*, 110; Parkinson, "Notes," *WHC*, 10:208; Ford, *History*, 216–17; Company of Vosburgh, May 15, 1832, *BHW*, 1:522–23; Thayer, *Battle of Wisconsin Heights*, 124–25; Clark to Clark, July 25, 1832, *BHW*, 2:877; Henry to Atkinson, July 23, 1832, *BHW*, 2:858.

95. Quoted from *Galenian*, August 1, 1832.

96. Axtell and Sturtevant, "Unkindest Cut," 451–72; Mooney, "Scalping," 482–83; Dodge to Atkinson, June 18, 1832, *BHW*, 2:623; Black Hawk, *Autobiography*, 143; Reynolds, *My Own Times*, 236; Examination of Prisoners, August 20, 1832, *BHW*, 2:1035; Statement of Munson, October 10–11, 1834, *BHW*, 2:1288; War News from Galena, May 30, 1832, *BHW*, 2:489, 490n.

97. Turner, *Red Men*, xiv–xv; Obsborn, *Wild Frontier*, 3–19, 38–40; quoted from Parkinson, "Pioneer," *WHC*, 2:356.

98. Parkinson, "Pioneer," *WHC*, 2:357; Wakefield, *History*, 110; Examination of Prisoners, August 19, 1832, *BHW*, 2:1028–29, 1031; Examination of Prisoners, August 20, 1832, *BHW*, 2:1035–37; Black Hawk, *Autobiography*, 155–57; Henry to Atkinson, July 23, 1832, *BHW*, 2:858; Thayer, *Battle of Wisconsin Heights*, 159.

99. Bracken, "Further Strictures," *WHC*, 2:408–09; Parkinson, "Pioneer," *WHC*, 2:358; Bracken, "Narrative," *HOW*, 220; quoted from Wakefield, *History*, 110.

100. Justice, Journal, *BHW*, 2:1325; Bracken, "Narrative," *HOW*, 220–21; Dickson, "Narrative," *WHC*, 5:316; Wakefield, *History*, 111; Parkinson, "Pioneer," *WHC*, 2:357; quoted from Magoon, "Memoirs," 431–32.

101. Bracken, "Further Strictures," *WHC*, 2:403, 409; *Vernon County Censor*, August 10, 1898; Dodge to Atkinson, July 22, 1832, *BHW*, 2:843; Black Hawk, *Autobiography*, 142–43; Stillman to the *Missouri Republican*, June 19, 1832, *BHW*, 2:636; Mahon, "Warfare," 260, 273; Magoon, "Memoirs," 432; quoted from Wakefield, *History*, 111.

102. Wakefield, *History*, 112; Bracken, "Narrative," *HOW*, 221; quoted from Black Hawk, *Autobiography*, 155.

103. Quoted from Chapman, "Early Events," *WHC*, 4:346.

104. Black Hawk, *Autobiography*, 155.

105. For the source that says the lead element's battle with the Indians began about 5:00 p.m., and which also states that Henry's regiments arrived an hour later, see Bracken, "Narrative," *HOW*, 221. Bracken repeated that Henry and his men arrived an hour later in Bracken, "Further Strictures," *WHC*, 2:409. For the source that states that Henry's regiments arrived only ten minutes after the battle commenced, see Parkinson, "Pioneer," *WHC*, 2:357–58.

106. Dodge to Atkinson, July 23, 1832, *BHW*, 2:843; Henry to Atkinson, July 23, 1832, *BHW*, 2:859; Black Hawk, *Autobiography*, 155; Wakefield, *History*, 111; Parkinson, "Pioneer," *WHC*, 2:357–58; Bracken, "Further Strictures," *WHC*, 2:409–10; Collins to unknown, July 25, 1832, *BHW*, 2:879; Magoon, "Memoirs," 432; Bracken, "Narrative," *HOW*, 221; Chapman, "Early Events," *WHC*, 4:346–47.

107. Henry to Atkinson, July 23, 1832, *BHW*, 2:859; Dodge to Atkinson, July 22, 1832, *BHW*, 2:843; Parkinson, "Strictures," *WHC*, 2:395–96; Bracken, "Further Strictures," *WHC*, 2:410–11; quoted from Hagan, "Dodge-Henry," 378, 382.

108. Dodge to Atkinson, July 23, 1832, *BHW*, 2:843; Henry to Atkinson, July 23, 1832, *BHW*, 2:859; Parkinson, "Pioneer," *WHC*, 2:358; Bracken, "Further Strictures," *WHC*, 2:409–10; quoted from Wakefield, *History*, 112.

109. Dodge to Atkinson, July 23, 1832, *BHW*, 2:843; Justice, Journal, *BHW*, 2:1325; Bracken, "Narrative," *HOW*, 221; Wakefield, *History*, 112; quoted from Bracken, "Further Strictures," *WHC*, 2:410.

110. Dodge to Atkinson, July 23, 1832, *BHW*, 2:843; Bracken, "Further Strictures," *WHC*, 2:410; Henry to Atkinson, July 23, 1832, *BHW*, 2:859; Wakefield, *History*, 112.

111. Clark to Clark, July 25, 1832, *BHW*, 2:877–78; Black Hawk, *Autobiography*, 155–56; Dodge to Atkinson, July 23, 1832, *BHW*, 2:843; *Galenian*, August 8, 1832; Parkinson, "Pioneer," *WHC*, 2:359; Estes, "Wisconsin Heights," *HOW*, 228–29; Thayer, *Battle of Wisconsin Heights*, 113, 156; Dodge to Atkinson, July 23, 1832, *BHW*, 2:843; Henry to Atkinson, July 23, 1832, *BHW*, 2:860; Wakefield, *History*, 113.

112. Dodge to Atkinson, July 23, 1832, *BHW*, 2:843, 844n; Henry to Atkinson, July 23, 1832, *BHW*, 2:860; Bracken, "Further Strictures," *WHC*, 2:410; Parkinson, "Pioneer," *WHC*, 2:358; Wakefield, *History*, 112–13; Magoon, "Memoirs," 432; Loomis to Atkinson, July 30–31, 1832, *BHW*, 2:907; Street to Atkinson, July 31, 1832, *BHW*, 2:908.

113. Quoted from Black Hawk, *Autobiography*, 155–56.

114. Kay, "Fur Trade," 275; Owen to Hogan and Huston, May 24, 1832, *BHW*, 2:431, 432n; Scott to Cass, August 19–21, 1832, *BHW*, 2:1025; Estes, "Battle of Wisconsin Heights," *HOW*, 228; Bracken, "Further Strictures," *WHC*, 2:406; Street to Atkinson, July 31, 1832, *BHW*, 2:908; Examination of Prisoners, August 27, 1832, *BHW*, 2:1056; Examination of Prisoners, August 20, 1832, *BHW*, 2:1037; Thayer, *Battle of Wisconsin Heights*, 156; quoted from Examination of Prisoners, August 19, 1832, *BHW*, 2:1028–29, 1033n.

115. Street to Atkinson, July 31, 1832, *BHW*, 2:909; quoted from Black Hawk, *Autobiography*, 156.

116. Decorah, "Narrative," *WHC*, 13:450–53; Examination of Prisoners, August 19, 1832, *BHW*, 2:1028–29; Examination of Prisoners, August 20, 1832, *BHW*, 2:1035–37; quoted from Black Hawk, *Autobiography*, 157.

117. Justice, Journal, *BHW*, 2:1325; Parkinson, "Pioneer," *WHC*, 2:359–60; quoted from Wakefield, *History*, 114–16.

118. Wakefield, *History*, 114–16, 134; *History of Jo Daviess County*, 294; Anderson, Memoranda, August 27, 1832, *BHW*, 2:1058; *Sangamo Journal*, August 25, 1832.

119. Wakefield, *History*, 117–18; Magoon, "Memoirs," 432; Johnston, Journal, July 21–24, 1832, *BHW*, 2:1318–19, 1319n; Justice, Journal, *BHW*, 2:1325; quoted from Atkinson to Scott, July 25, 1832, *BHW*, 2:875.

Chapter 5

120. Atkinson to Scott, July 27, 1832, *BHW*, 2:891; Johnston, Journal, July 24–28, 1832, *BHW*, 2:1319; Libby, "Helena Shot-Tower," *WHC*, 13:341–42; Return of Illinois Mounted Volunteers, August 2, 1832, *BHW*, 1:574; Justice, Journal, *BHW*, 2:1325; Examination of Prisoners, August 27, 1832, *BHW*, 2:1056; Wakefield, *History*, 121–28; Cooke, *Scenes and Adventures*, 171–80; [Smith], "Indian Campaign," 329–30.

121. Johnston, Journal, August 1, 1832, *BHW*, 2:1320; Wakefield, *History*, 128; Loomis to Dodge, July 25, 1832, *BHW*, 2:880–81; Atkinson to Scott, August 5, 1832, *BHW*, 2:936; Burnett to Street, July 26, 1832, *BHW*, 2:883; Burnett to Street, July 28, 1832, *BHW*, 2:898–99; Loomis to Atkinson, July 30–31, 1832, *BHW*, 2:906–07; Throckmorton, Report, August 3, 1832, *BHW*, 2:927–28; Abercrombie to Loomis, August 8, 1832, *BHW*, 2:960; Street to Atkinson, July 31, 1832, *BHW*, 2:908–09.

122. Holmes to Atkinson, August 5, 1832, *BHW*, 2:938; Street to Clark, August 2, 1832, *BHW*, 2:917; Atkinson to Boyd, July 12, 1832, *BHW*, 2:770–71; Boyd to Atkinson, July 20, 1832, *BHW*, 2:834; Roll of Johnston's Company, July 20–August 28, 1832, Baird MSS, 5:4, Roll of Grignon's Company, July 20–August 28, 1832, Baird MSS, 5:4; Boyd to Stambaugh's staff, July 24, 1832, *WHC*, 12:281.

123. Jung, *Black Hawk War*, 170, 165–66, 179–80; Fonda, "Reminiscences," *WHC*, 5:261; Throckmorton, Report, August 3, 1832, *BHW*, 2:927–28; Black Hawk, *Autobiography*, 158–60; Examination of Prisoners, August 19, 1932, *BHW*, 2:1029; Holmes to Atkinson, August 5, 1832, *BHW*, 2:938–39.

124. Johnston, Journal, August 1–2, 1832, *BHW*, 2:1320; Jung, *Black Hawk War*, 168–69; quoted from Black Hawk, *Autobiography*, 160.

125. Black Hawk, *Autobiography*, 160–62; Dickson, "Narrative," *WHC*, 5:316; Examination of Prisoners, August 19, 1832, *BHW*, 2:1031; Atkinson to Scott, August 9, 1832, *BHW*, 2:965; Johnston, Journal, August 2, 1832, *BHW*, 2:1320–21; *De Soto Chronicle*, January 29, 1887; Jung, *Black Hawk War*, 168–69; quoted from Examination of Prisoners, August 27, 1832, *BHW*, 2:1056.

126. Atkinson to Scott, August 9, 1832, *BHW*, 2:965; War News from Galena, August 6, 1832, *BHW*, 2:954–55; Zachary Taylor, Report, August 5, 1832, *BHW*, 2:942; Fonda, "Reminiscences," *WHC*, 5:262.

127. Atkinson to Scott, August 9, 1832, *BHW*, 2:965; Wakefield, *History*, 131–34; Justice, Journal, *BHW*, 2:1326; quoted from *Vernon County Censor*, August 10, 1898.

128. *De Soto Chronicle*, February 12, 1887; quoted from Perrin, *History*, 231–32.

129. *De Soto Chronicle*, February 12, 1887.

130. [Smith], "Indian Campaign," 331; Johnston, Journal, August 2, 1832, *BHW*, 2:1321; Eaton, "Returns," 37; Jung, *Black Hawk War*, 172.

131. Scott to Cass, August 10, 1832, *BHW*, 2:980; Street to Scott, August 22, 1832, *BHW*, 2:1041–42; Stambaugh to Scott, August 11, 1832, *BHW*, 2:987; Stambaugh to Boyd, August 28, 1832, *BHW*, 2:1071–78; Street to Scott, August 22, 1832, *BHW*, 2:1042.

132. Scott to Cass, August 19, 1832, *BHW*, 2:1025; Preliminary Roll of Prisoners, August 27, 1832, *BHW*, 2:1058–61; Roll of Prisoners at Rock Island, August 27, 1832, *BHW*, 2:1062–65; Black Hawk, *Autobiography*, 161n; Jung, *Black Hawk War*, 172, 174, 179.

133. Lurie, "Chaetar," 163–83; Black Hawk, *Autobiography*, 162–63; Street, Report of Delivery of Black Hawk and Prophet, August 27, 1832, *BHW*, 2:1065–67; *Galenian*, September 5, 1832; Scanlan, "Jefferson Davis," 174–82.

134. Scott to Taylor, September 5, 1832, *BHW*, 2:1111; Council with Sauk and Fox, September 19, 1832, *BHW*, 2:1168; Roll of Prisoners at Rock Island, August 27, 1832, *BHW*, 2:1062–64; *Galenian*, September 5, 1832; Anderson to Anderson, September 9, 1832, *BHW*, 2:1121–22; quoted from Black Hawk, *Autobiography*, 165–66.

135. Atkinson to Scott, September 16, 1832, *BHW*, 2:1157; Black Hawk, *Autobiography*, 1–7, 7n, 166; Atkinson to Macomb, April 5, 1832, A51-1833.

136. Nichols, *Black Hawk*, 146–47; Black Hawk, *Autobiography*, 167–70; Turner, *Red Men*, 91–93; *National Intelligencer*, April 29, 1833.

137. Treadway, "Triumph," 8–13; Nichols, *Black Hawk*, 147–48.

138. Treadway, "Triumph," 14–15; quoted from Black Hawk, *Autobiography*, 172.

139. Treadway, "Triumph," 15; Black Hawk, *Autobiography*, 172–74.

140. Treadway, "Triumph," 15–16; quoted from Garland to Cass, October 5, 1832, M-234, 728:405–06.

141. Black Hawk, *Autobiography*, 176–77; Nichols, *Black Hawk*, 150–54.

142. Black Hawk, *Autobiography*, 175; Councils with Sauk and Fox, September 19–21, 1832, *BHW*, 2:1166–80; Treaty with Sauks and Foxes, September 21, 1832, *IALT*, 349–51; Councils with Winnebagos, September 10–12, 1832, *BHW*, 2:1130–35; Treaty with Winnebago, September 15, 1832, *IALT*, 345–48; Royce, "Indian Land Cessions," 736–37.

143. Quoted from Black Hawk, *Autobiography*, 31–38, 181–82.

EPILOGUE

144. Quoted from Catlin, *Letters and Notes*, 217.

145. Quoted from Smith, "Journal," 211–12.

146. Quoted from Marsh, "Expedition," *WHC*, 15:117.

147. Quoted from Black Hawk, *Autobiography*, 156.

148. Quoted from Cooke, *Scenes and Adventures*, 171.

149. Quoted from Aldrich, "Jefferson Davis," 409.

150. Titus, "Wisconsin Heights," 55–60; *Baraboo Daily News*, November 12, 1919; quoted from Titus, "Sauk City," 332–39.

151. Quoted from [Schafer], "Field Meetings," 250.

Works Cited

MANUSCRIPT COLLECTIONS

Baird, Henry S. Papers. Wisconsin Historical Society, Madison, Wisconsin.

Boilvin, Nicholas. Letters, 1811–1823. In Prairie du Chien, Wisconsin Papers. University of Wisconsin–Platteville, Area Research Center, Platteville, Wisconsin.

Forsyth, Thomas. Papers. Series T, Lyman C. Draper Manuscript Collection. Wisconsin Historical Society, Madison, Wisconsin.

Michelson, Truman. Notes on Sauk Ethnography, MS 2735. National Anthropological Archives, National Museum of Natural History, Smithsonian Institution, Washington, D.C.

Taliaferro, Lawrence. Papers. Minnesota Historical Society, Minneapolis, Minnesota.

UNPUBLISHED PUBLIC RECORDS

Adjutant General's Office. Letters Received by the Office of the Adjutant General, 1805–1899. RG 94, Records of the Office of the Adjutant General. National Archives, Washington, D.C.

———. Returns from U.S. Military Posts, 1800–1916. Microfilm Publication M-617. RG 94, Records of the Office of the Adjutant General. National Archives, Washington, D.C.

Bureau of Indian Affairs. Documents Relating to the Negotiation of Ratified and Unratified Treaties with Various Tribes of Indians, 1801–1869. Microfilm Publication T-494. RG 75, Records of the Bureau of Indian Affairs. National Archives, Washington, D.C.

———. Letters Received by the Office of Indian Affairs, 1824–1881. Microfilm Publication M-234. RG 75, Records of the Bureau of Indian Affairs. National Archives, Washington, D.C.

———. Letters Sent by the Office of Indian Affairs, 1824–1881. Microfilm Publication M-21. RG 75, Records of the Bureau of Indian Affairs. National Archives, Washington, D.C.

———. Records of the Michigan Superintendency of Indian Affairs, 1814–1851. Microfilm Publication M-1. RG 75, Records of the Bureau of Indian Affairs. National Archives, Washington, D.C.

Eaton, J.H. "Returns of the Killed and Wounded of American Troops in Battles or Engagements with the Indians." RG 94, Records of the Office of the Adjutant General. National Archives, Washington, D.C.

Indian Claims Commission. Docket 83, Sac and Fox Indians. RG 279, Records of the Indian Claims Commission. National Archives, Washington, D.C.

PUBLISHED PUBLIC RECORDS

American State Papers: Indian Affairs. 2 vols. Washington, D.C.: Gales and Seaton, 1832–1834.

Davis, J.C. Bancroft, ed. *Treaties and Conventions Concluded between the United States of American and Other Powers since July 4, 1776*. Washington, D.C.: Government Printing Office, 1873.

Kappler, Charles J., ed. *Indian Affairs: Laws and Treaties*. Vol. 2. Washington, D.C.: Government Printing Office, 1904.

War Department. *Annual Report of the Secretary of War for 1827*. 20th Cong., 1st sess., 1827. Ho. Doc. 2. Serial 169.

———. *Annual Report of the Secretary of War for 1828*. 20th Cong., 2nd sess., 1828, Sen. Doc. 1. Serial 181.

———. *Letter from the Secretary of War.* 20th Cong., 1st sess., 1828. Ho. Doc. 277. Serial 175.

PUBLISHED PRIMARY SOURCES

Aldrich, Charles. "Jefferson Davis and Black Hawk." *Midland Monthly* 5 (May 1896): 406–11.

Atwater, Caleb. *Remarks on a Tour to Prairie du Chien Thence to Washington City in 1829*. Columbus, OH: Isaac N. Whiting, 1831.

[Backus, Electus]. "A Brief History of the War with the Sac & Fox Indians." In *Collections of the Michigan Pioneer and Historical Society*. Vol. 12, 424–36. Lansing: Michigan Pioneer and Historical Society, 1888.

Basler, Roy P., ed. *Collected Works of Abraham Lincoln*. 9 vols. New Brunswick, NJ: Rutgers University Press, 1953–55.

Black Hawk. *Black Hawk: An Autobiography*. Edited by Donald Jackson. 1833. Reprint, Urbana: University of Illinois Press, 1955.

Bracken, Charles. "Further Strictures Upon Ford's Black Hawk War." In *Collections of the State Historical Society of Wisconsin*. Vol. 2, 402–14. Madison: State Historical Society of Wisconsin, 1903.

———. "Personal Narrative of Charles Bracken." In *The History of Wisconsin. In Three Parts*. Vol. 3, 215–23. Edited by William Smith. Madison, WI: Beriah Brown, 1854.

WORKS CITED

Carter, Clarence E., and John P. Bloom, eds. *The Territorial Papers of the United States.* 28 vols. Washington, D.C.: Government Printing Office, 1934–75.

Catlin, George. *Letters and Notes on the Manners, Customs, and Condition of the North American Indians.* Vol. 2. New York: Wiley and Putnam, 1841.

Chapman, C.D. "Early Events in the Four Lake Country." In *Collections of the State Historical Society of Wisconsin.* Vol. 4, 343–49. Madison: State Historical Society of Wisconsin, 1906.

Childs, Ebenezer. "Recollections of Wisconsin since 1820." In *Collections of the State Historical Society of Wisconsin.* Vol. 4, 153–95. Madison: State Historical Society of Wisconsin, 1906.

Cooke, Philip S. *Scenes and Adventures in the Army, Or the Romance of Military Life.* Philadelphia: Lindsay & Blakiston, 1857.

Decorah, Spoon. "Narrative of Spoon Decorah." In *Collections of the State Historical Society of Wisconsin.* Vol. 13, 448–62. Madison: State Historical Society of Wisconsin, 1895.

De La Ronde, John T. "Personal Narrative." In *Collections of the State Historical Society of Wisconsin.* Vol. 7, 345–65. Madison: State Historical Society of Wisconsin, 1908.

Dickson, Joseph. "Personal Narratives." In *Collections of the State Historical Society of Wisconsin.* Vol. 5, 315–17. Madison: State Historical Society of Wisconsin, 1907.

Draper, Lyman C., et al., eds. *Collections of the State Historical Society of Wisconsin.* 31 vols. Madison: State Historical Society of Wisconsin, 1855–1931.

Esarey, Logan, ed. *Messages and Letters of William Henry Harrison.* 2 vols. *Indiana Historical Collections,* vols. 7 and 9. Indianapolis: Indiana Historical Commission, 1922.

Estes, James B. "Battle of Wisconsin Heights." In *The History of Wisconsin. In Three Parts.* Vol. 3, 228–30. Edited by William Smith. Madison, WI: Beriah Brown, 1854.

Fonda, John H. "Early Reminiscences of Wisconsin." In *Collections of the State Historical Society of Wisconsin.* Vol. 5, 205–84. Madison: State Historical Society of Wisconsin, 1907.

Ford, Thomas. *A History of Illinois.* Edited by Milo M. Quaife. 1854. Reprint, Chicago: Lakeside Press, 1945.

General Regulations for the Army; Or, Military Institutes. Philadelphia: M. Carey and Sons, 1821.

The History of Jo Daviess County Illinois. Chicago: H.F. Kett & Co., 1878.

Holmes, J.C., et al., eds. *Collections of the Michigan Pioneer and Historical Society.* 40 vols. Lansing: Michigan Pioneer and Historical Society, 1877–1929.

Iles, Elijah. *Sketches of Early Life and Times in Kentucky, Missouri, and Illinois.* Springfield, IL: Springfield Printing Co., 1883.

Magoon, R.H. "R.H. Magoon's Memoirs." In *History of Grant County, Wisconsin,* 427–35. Chicago: Western Historical Company, 1881.

Marsh, Cutting. "Expedition to the Sauks and Foxes." In *Collections of the State Historical Society of Wisconsin.* Vol. 15, 104–55. Madison: State Historical Society of Wisconsin, 1900.

Matson, Nehemiah. *Memories of Shaubena, With Incidents Relating to the Early Settlement of the West.* Chicago: D.B. Cooke and Co., 1878.

McKenney, Thomas L. *Memoirs Official and Personal.* 2nd ed. New York: Paine and Burgess, 1846.

Ogden, George W. "Narrative of George W. Ogden." In *History of Rock County, and Transactions of the Rock County Agricultural Society and Mechanics Institute*, 41–43. Edited by Orrin Guernsey and Josiah Willard. Janesville, WI: William M. Doty and Brother, 1856.

Parkinson, Daniel M. "Pioneer Life in Wisconsin." In *Collections of the State Historical Society of Wisconsin*. Vol. 2, 326–64. Madison: State Historical Society of Wisconsin, 1903.

Parkinson, Peter, Jr. "Notes on the Black Hawk War." In *Collections of the State Historical Society of Wisconsin*. Vol. 10, 184–212. Madison: State Historical Society of Wisconsin, 1909.

———. "Strictures Upon Ford's Black Hawk War." In *Collections of the State Historical Society of Wisconsin*. Vol. 2, 393–401. Madison: State Historical Society of Wisconsin, 1903.

Perrin, William H., ed. *History of Crawford and Clark Counties, Illinois*. Chicago: O.L. Baskin & Co., 1882.

Quaife, Milton M., ed. *The Early Day of Rock Island and Davenport: The Narratives of J.W. Spencer and J.M.D. Burrows*. Chicago: Lakeside Press, 1942.

Reynolds, John. *My Own Times: Embracing a History of My Life*. Chicago: Chicago Historical Society, 1879.

Rising, Marsha, ed. "White Claims for Indian Depredations: Illinois-Missouri-Arkansas Frontier, 1804–32." *National Genealogical Society Quarterly* 84 (December 1996): 274–304.

[Schafer, Joseph]. "Field Meetings." *Wisconsin Magazine of History* 7 (December 1923): 249–50.

[Smith, Henry]. "Indian Campaign of 1832." *Military and Naval Magazine of the United States* 1 (August 1833): 321–33.

Smith, William R. "Journal of William Rudolph Smith." Edited by Joseph Schafer. *Wisconsin Magazine of History* 12 (December 1928): 192–220.

Taylor, Zachary. "Zachary Taylor in Illinois." Edited by Holman Hamilton. *Journal of the Illinois State Historical Society* 34 (March 1941): 84–91.

Thayer, Crawford B., ed. *Hunting a Shadow: An Eye-Witness Account of the Black Hawk War of 1832*. Menasha, WI: Banta Press, 1981.

———. *The Battle of Wisconsin Heights: An Eye-Witness Account of the Black Hawk War of 1832*. Menasha, WI: Banta Press, 1983.

Wakefield, John. *Wakefield's History of the Black Hawk War*. Edited by Frank Stevens. 1834. Reprint, Madison, WI: Roger Hunt, 1976.

Whitney, Ellen M., ed. *The Black Hawk War, 1831–1832*. 2 vols. *Collections of the Illinois Historical Library*, vols. 35–38. Springfield: Illinois Historical Library, 1970–78.

Wilson, Douglas L., and Rodney O. Davis, eds. *Herndon's Informants: Letters, Interviews, and Statements about Abraham Lincoln*. Urbana: University of Illinois Press, 1998.

NEWSPAPERS

Baraboo Daily News [Baraboo, WI], 1919.
De Soto Chronicle [De Soto, WI], 1887.
Galenian [Galena, IL], 1832.

WORKS CITED

Missouri Gazette [St. Louis, MO], 1815–16.
Missouri Gazette and Illinois Advertiser [St. Louis, MO], 1815.
National Intelligencer [Washington, D.C.], 1833.
Niles Weekly Register [Baltimore, MD], 1832–33.
Sangamo Journal [Springfield, IL], 1832.
Vernon County Censor [Vernon, WI], 1898.

SECONDARY SOURCES

Allen, Robert S. *His Majesty's Indian Allies: British Indian Policy in the Defence of Canada, 1774–1815.* Toronto: Dundurn Press, 1992.

Armstrong, Perry A. *The Sauks and the Black Hawk War.* Springfield, IL: H.W. Rokker, 1887.

Axtell, James, and William C. Sturtevant. "The Unkindest Cut, or, Who Invented Scalping?" *William and Mary Quarterly* 37 (July 1980): 451–72.

Barton, A.O. "Black Hawk Retreat in Dane County." *Wisconsin Archeologist* 24 (December 1943): 61–67.

Callender, Charles. "Fox." In *Handbook of North American Indians.* Vol. 15, *Northeast*, 648–55. Edited by Bruce Trigger. Washington, D.C.: Smithsonian Institution, 1978.

———. "Great Lakes-Riverine Sociopolitical Organization." In *Handbook of North American Indians.* Vol. 15, *Northeast*, 610–21. Edited by Bruce Trigger. Washington, D.C.: Smithsonian Institution, 1978.

———. "Sauk." In *Handbook of North American Indians.* Vol. 15, *Northeast*, 636–47. Edited by Bruce Trigger. Washington, D.C.: Smithsonian Institution, 1978.

Clifton, James. *The Prairie People: Continuity and Change in Potawatomi Indian Culture, 1665–1965.* Lawrence: Regents Press of Kansas, 1977.

Cummings, J.E. "The Burning of Sauk-E-Nuk: The Westernmost Battle of the Revolution." *Journal of the Illinois State Historical Society* 20 (April 1927): 49–62.

Dowd, Gregory. *A Spirited Resistance: The North American Indian Struggle for Unity, 1745–1815.* Baltimore: Johns Hopkins University Press, 1992.

Eby, Cecil. *"That Disgraceful Affair": The Black Hawk War.* New York: W.W. Norton and Co., 1973.

Edmunds, R. David, and Joseph L. Peyser, *The Fox Wars: The Mesquakie Challenge to New France.* Norman: University of Oklahoma Press, 1993.

Eid, Leroy. "'National' War among Indians of Northeastern North America." *Canadian Review of American Studies* 16 (Summer 1985): 125–54.

Everhart, Duane. "The Leasing of Mineral Lands in Illinois and Wisconsin." *Journal of the Illinois Historical Society* 60 (Summer 1967): 117–36.

Fisher, Robert L. "The Treaties of Portage des Sioux." *Mississippi Valley Historical Review* 19 (March 1933): 495–508.

Fiske, John. *The American Revolution.* Cambridge, MA: Riverside Press, 1919.

Foley, William. "Different Notions of Justice: The Case of the 1808 St. Louis Murder Trials." *Gateway Heritage* 9 (Winter 1988–89): 2–13.

Gibson, A.M. *The Kickapoos: Lords of the Middle Border.* Norman: University of Oklahoma Press, 1963.

WORKS CITED

Gilpin, Alec R. *The War of 1812 in the Old Northwest*. East Lansing: Michigan State University Press, 1958.

Hagan, William T. "The Dodge-Henry Controversy." *Journal of the Illinois State Historical Society* 50 (Winter 1957): 377–84.

———. "General Henry Atkinson and the Militia." *Military Affairs* 23 (Winter 1959–60): 194–97.

———. *The Sac and Fox Indians*. Norman: University of Oklahoma Press, 1958.

Hall, John W. *Uncommon Defense: Indian Allies in the Black Hawk War*. Cambridge, MA: Harvard University Press, 2009.

Hauberg, John. "The Black Hawk War, 1831–1832." In *Transactions of the Illinois State Historical Society, 1932*, 91–134. Springfield: Illinois State Historical Society, 1932.

Hickerson, Harold. *The Chippewa and Their Neighbors: A Study in Ethnohistory*. New York: Holt, Rhinehart and Winston, 1970.

Horsman, Reginald. *Expansion and American Indian Policy, 1783–1812*. East Lansing: Michigan State University Press, 1967.

———. "Wisconsin and the War of 1812." *Wisconsin Magazine of History* 46 (Autumn 1962): 3–15.

Jackson, Donald. "Old Fort Madison—1808–1813." *Palimpsest* 47 (January 1966): 1–62.

Jones, William. *Ethnography of the Fox Indians*. Washington, D.C.: Government Printing Office, 1939.

Jung, Patrick J. *The Black Hawk War of 1832*. Norman: University of Oklahoma Press, 2007.

Kay, Jeanne. "The Fur Trade and Native American Population Growth." *Ethnohistory* 31 (Autumn 1984): 265–87.

Kuhm, Herbert W. "The Mining and Use of Lead by the Wisconsin Indians." *Wisconsin Archeologist* 32 (June 1951): 25–37.

Libby, Orin G. "Chronicle of the Helena Shot-Tower." In *Collections of the State Historical Society of Wisconsin*. Vol. 13, 335–74. Madison: State Historical Society of Wisconsin, 1909.

Lurie, Nancy O. "In Search of Chaetar: New Findings on Black Hawk's Surrender." *Wisconsin Magazine of History* 71 (Spring 1988): 163–83.

Mahon, John K. "Anglo-American Methods of Indian Warfare, 1676–1794." *Mississippi Valley Historical Review* 45 (September 1958): 254–75.

Mayne, D.D. "The Old Fort at Fort Atkinson." In *Proceedings of the State Historical Society of Wisconsin, 1898*, 197–201. Madison, WI: Democrat Printing Co., 1899.

Metcalf, P. Richard. "Who Should Rule at Home? Native American Politics and Indian White Relations." *Journal of American History* 61 (December 1974): 651–65.

Mooney, James. "Scalping." In *Handbook of American Indians North of Mexico*. Vol. 2, 482–483. Edited by Frederick Hodge. Washington, D.C.: Government Printing Office, 1910.

Nichols, Roger L. *Black Hawk and the Warrior's Path*. Arlington Heights, IL: Harlan Davidson, 1992.

———. "General Henry Atkinson and the Building of Jefferson Barracks." *Bulletin of the Missouri Historical Society* 22 (April 1966): 321–26.

————. *General Henry Atkinson: A Western Military Career*. Norman: University of Oklahoma Press, 1965.

Obsborn, William M. *The Wild Frontier: Atrocities during the American Indian Wars from Jamestown Colony to Wounded Knee*. New York: Random House, 2000.

Ourada, Patricia K. *The Menominee Indians: A History*. Norman: University of Oklahoma Press, 1979.

Pelzer, Louis. *Henry Dodge*. Iowa City: State Historical Society of Iowa, 1911.

Prucha, Francis Paul. *The Great Father: The United States Government and the American Indians*. 2 vols. Lincoln: University of Nebraska Press, 1984.

Scanlan, P.L. "The Military Record of Jefferson Davis in Wisconsin." *Wisconsin Magazine of History* 24 (December 1940): 174–82.

Silver, James. *Edmund Pendleton Gaines: Frontier General*. Baton Rouge: Louisiana State University Press, 1949.

Skinner, Alanson. *Observations on the Ethnology of the Sauk Indians*. Milwaukee: Milwaukee Public Museum, 1923.

Starkey, Armstrong. *European and Native American Warfare, 1675–1815*. Norman: University of Oklahoma Press, 1998.

Stevens, Frank. *The Black Hawk War*. Chicago: Blakely Printing Company, 1903.

————. "A Forgotten Hero: General James Dougherty Henry." In *Transactions of the Illinois State Historical Society, 1934*, 77–120. Springfield: Illinois State Historical Library, 1934.

————. "Illinois in the War of 1812–1814." In *Transactions of the Illinois State Historical Society, 1904*, 62–197. Springfield: Illinois State Historical Library, 1904.

Suppinger, Joseph. "Private Lincoln and the Spy Battalion." *Lincoln Herald* 80 (Spring 1978): 46–49.

Tanner, Helen Hornbeck, ed. *Atlas of Great Lakes Indian History*. Norman: University of Oklahoma Press, 1987.

Thian, Raphael P. *Notes Illustrating the Military Geography of the United States, 1813–1880*. Washington, D.C.: Government Printing Office, 1881.

Titus, W.A. "Historic Spots in Wisconsin: The Battle of Wisconsin Heights." *Wisconsin Magazine of History* 4 (December 1920): 55–60.

————. "Historic Spots in Wisconsin: Sauk City and Prairie du Sac, Twin Villages with an Historic Background." *Wisconsin Magazine of History* 9 (March 1926): 332–39.

Trask, Kerry. *Black Hawk: The Battle for the Heart of America*. New York: Henry Holt and Company, 2006.

Treadway, Sandra G. "Triumph in Defeat: Black Hawk's 1833 Visit to Virginia." *Virginia Cavalcade* 35 (Summer 1985): 4–17.

Turner, Andrew Jackson. "The History of Fort Winnebago." In *Collections of the State Historical Society of Wisconsin*. Vol. 14, 65–102. Madison: State Historical Society of Wisconsin, 1898.

Turner, Katharine C. *Red Men Calling on the Great White Father*. Norman: University of Oklahoma Press, 1951.

Wallace, Anthony F.C. *Jefferson and the Indians: The Tragic Fate of the First Americans*. Cambridge, MA: Belknap, 1999.

Works Cited

————. "Prelude to Disaster: The Course of Indian-White Relations Which Led to the Black Hawk War of 1832." In *The Black Hawk War, 1831–1832*. Vol. 1, 1–51. Edited by Ellen M. Whitney. *Collections of the Illinois State Historical Library*, vol. 35. Springfield: Illinois State Historical Library, 1970.

White, Richard. *The Middle Ground: Indians, Empires, and Republics in the Great Lakes Region, 1650–1815*. New York: Cambridge University Press, 1991.

Zanger, Martin. "Conflicting Concepts of Justice: A Winnebago Murder Trial on the Illinois Frontier." *Journal of the Illinois State Historical Society* 73 (Winter 1980): 263–76.

————. "Pierre Paquette, Winnebago Mixed-Blood: Profiteer or Tribal Spokesman?" In *Anthology of Western Great Lakes Indian History*. Edited by Donald Fixico. Milwaukee: University of Wisconsin-Milwaukee Indian Studies, 1987.

————. "Red Bird." In *American Indian Leaders: Studies in Diversity*. Edited by R. David Edmunds. Lincoln: University of Nebraska Press, 1980.

Dissertations

Kurtz, Royce D. "Economic and Political History of the Sauk and Mesquakie: 1780s–1845." PhD diss., University of Iowa, 1986.

Sims, Catherine A. "Algonkian-British Relations in the Upper Great Lakes Region: Gathering to Give and Receive Presents, 1815–1843." PhD diss., University of Western Ontario, 1992.

Index

About the Author

D r. Patrick Jung teaches history at the Milwaukee School of Engineering and is the author of *The Black Hawk War of 1832*.

Visit us at
www.historypress.net

www.ingramcontent.com/pod-product-compliance
Lightning Source LLC
Chambersburg PA
CBHW071150160426
42812CB00079B/1492